THIS FOR THE HALF

Keith B. Marshall's golf writing gave much pleasure in the columns of *Golf Monthly*, in which all the selected pieces included in *This for the Half* originally appeared. His association with the magazine spans four decades and he was one of its regular columnists. He was a freelance writer and author of a previous book, *Golf Galore*, his articles have been published at home and abroad.

With Cartoons by ROD McLEOD

THIS FOR THE HALF

KEITH B. MARSHALL

A SPHERE BOOK

SPHERE BOOKS LTD

First published in Great Britain
by Robert Hale Limited 1988
Published by Sphere Books Limited 1989

ISBN 0 7474 0430 5

Printed and bound in Great Britain by
Cox & Wyman Ltd, Reading

Sphere Books Ltd
A Division of
Macdonald & Co (Publishers) Ltd
66–73 Shoe Lane
London EC4P 4AB
A member of Maxwell Pergamon Publishing Corporation plc

Contents

Foreword

by
Malcolm Campbell

According to the paid-up disciples of Murphy's Law, golf is neither a game of skill nor of chance, but simply a vicious, no-holds-barred struggle against the principle that if anything can go wrong it undoubtedly will. However, those of us who fall some way short of that essentially false but understandable philosophy, know that the royal and ancient game is a rich source of great enjoyment and much humour. Its followers are fortunate in that their chosen sport is perhaps better served in the distillation of these vital ingredients by its writers than almost any other.

I commend this volume to you in the firm belief that there are few who have a sharper pen for this distillation process than its author, Keith B. Marshall. Within these covers you will find a rare combination of humour, tuition and wisdom, complemented perfectly by the drawings of Rod McLeod.

Over many years Mr Marshall has been a valued contributor to *Golf Monthly* and, indeed, this volume is an assembly of some fifty articles which have at one time or another appeared exclusively in the magazine's columns. Their compilation in a separate volume was long overdue and, if you enjoy them as much as I have, you will, I am sure, be well pleased.

In reading *This for the Half*, you will also have discovered the ultimate Law of Murphy, the Apotheosis of Golf: for golf is not a game, it is a way of life, and we pass along its tortuous and humorous path alas but once.

M.C.

To Kathy with love

The only partner in whom I met my match –
and lost to *willingly*.

Preface and Acknowledgements

This for the Half is a collection of articles which have appeared in *Golf Monthly*, to which I have contributed for many years. My thanks go to the editor, Malcolm Campbell, and the magazine's proprietors.

Within these pages, fact, fiction and occasional fantasy are interwoven and many intriguing questions answered. For example, why are so many golfers standing on one leg? Why do others risk the displeasure of the domestic side of the household by swinging the kitchen broom? Why are golfers henpecked? Why is golf played by the light of the moon, and what is – or was – the Utopian golfing residence?

In this get-together of golfing miscellany, Jack Nicklaus rolls up his pants and splashes out of water; Arnold Palmer and Bernhard Langer shin up trees and, spiking themselves within the branches, whack manfully back to play. The legendary Bobby Jones, briefly forsaking the fairway, finds his ball in an old shoe in a wheelbarrow but, undeterred, socks ball and shoe onto the green. For strictly personal reasons, Jimmy Braid keeps his eye on the big drum, and Bobby Clampett compares himself to a duck.

I have enjoyed putting this book together and becoming re-acquainted with writing scattered about like practice shots on the fairway, some of which I had almost forgotten. Similarly, I hope my readers will enjoy themselves and perhaps try out a few of the golfing tips, none of which is complex or technical.

Why (since I am bound to be asked) the title – *This for the Half*? Well, a hole is halved when each side holes out in the same number of strokes, and games are halved when each side wins the same number of holes. In like manner, a book is shared by reader and author, and all chapters may be looked upon as halved, with the match ending all square. If we then go on to the 19th, it will not be to reach a golfing decision but to raise our glasses and say 'THIS FOR THE HALF!'

Acknowledgements and thanks for the use of copyright material are given to the undermentioned:

W.H. Allen & Co. Plc for *A-Sitting on a Gate* by Ben Travers; Chapman & Hall Ltd for *The Common Touch* by James Agate; Chatto & Windus Ltd for *Golf is My Game* by Bobby Jones; Enid Wilson for *A Gallery of Women Golfers*; André Deutsch Ltd for *The Bogey Man* by George Plimpton; Harrap Ltd for *The Selective Ego* by James Agate; Hutchinson Publishing Group Ltd for *Express and Admirable* by James Agate, *The Golf Omnibus* by P.G. Wodehouse, and *Miss Mapp* by E.F. Benson; Sidgwick & Jackson Ltd for *The Game's Afoot* by Bernard Darwin and others; Simon & Schuster Inc for *The Walter Hagen Story* by Walter Hagen and Margaret Seaton Heck; A.P. Watt Ltd on behalf of the Estate of Gerard Fairlie for *With Prejudice* by Gerard Fairlie.

1 The Wilderness of Superiority

'Why does golf make some men so intolerable?' asked E.V. Lucas. 'Not all, of course, but too many. Why is it that one would rather walk home than sit in a railway compartment amid a certain type of golfer? What is there about golf to so lift a man's nose, and curl his lip, and steel his manners, and doom him to dwell in the wilderness of superiority?'

Golfers have changed since E.V. Lucas wrote that. Instead of sitting in railway compartments, they make prodigious drives up long motorways, and each and every one would turn a whiter shade of pale at the mere thought of walking home. Indeed, there are some who don't even *walk* on the course itself, but ride from tee to green in buggies with a fringe on top. But what of *the wilderness of superiority*? Are noses still lifted and lips curled? I hardly think so. Time – like the ever-rolling bulldozer – is a great leveller, and the only similarity between the turn-of-the-century golfer and today's Herbert is that he still has that nasty habit of telling us golf stories that we've heard a million times before.

One golfer who dwelled in a wilderness of superiority was written about by Gerard Fairlie, journalist, novelist and screenwriter, whose grandfather, Colonel Fairlie, is said to have played golf (like Groucho Marx) with a large cigar in his mouth. He it was who taught Old Tom Morris to smoke after taking him from St Andrews to be keeper of the links at Prestwick. No low-to-middle tar or Government health warning prompted second thoughts then!

Fairlie's story was of an extraordinary incident that occurred when he was playing a practice round at Deauville. He was at the first tee, waiting his turn to drive off, when a single player – a Frenchman – appeared on the tee and, without saying a word

13

to anyone, drove his ball straight down the middle of the fairway.

In no particular hurry to play, Fairlie – somewhat uncertain of the standing of a single player at Deauville – raised no objection, and merely waited patiently until the Frenchman had played his second shot to the green.

The first at Deauville being an easy four, the Frenchman put his ball on the green, whereupon Fairlie and his companions drove off, and then stood waiting for him to putt out and move off towards the second tee.

But Fairlie described how the Frenchman then did a very odd thing. 'He teed his ball on the near edge of the green and took up his stance as if to drive straight back at us. Before we had recovered from our astonishment, he actually did so. A well-hit ball soared away over our heads. He then started to advance straight down the fairway towards us.'

Fairlie had no idea what to do. The situation was so bizarre and beyond understanding that he didn't know whether to shout 'Fore!' or ask politely if they might go through. However, as the Frenchman approached, Fairlie saw that he was extremely angry. He walked straight up and said: 'Sir, I have paid my green fee; I have selected this hole. There are seventeen others. Go to one of them!'

The wilderness of superiority, in a somewhat different context, occurred when Fairlie took a team of golfers to France, which he used to do annually. It was his privilege to sit next to the President of the club during dinner and, in the course of conversation, he began to realize that the President knew nothing of the game; when he was asked what he thought of the course, he replied quite truthfully that it was one of the most delightful he had played – but he added a small criticism by saying that, if the course had a fault, it was perhaps a trifle short.

'Ah,' said the President, 'too short.' And then he asked Fairlie how many holes there were. Rather surprised, Fairlie answered that there were the normal eighteen.

'Too short,' said the President firmly. 'Thank you for telling me. We will have twenty.'

One golfer who was in a wilderness of superiority all of his own was Tommy Bolt, American Ryder Cup star and former US Open champion. For when it came to throwing clubs and breaking them in temperamental outbursts, Tommy was superior to all others.

That Bolt's temper often got the better of him, I can personally confirm. I walked with him during his singles match against the great Scottish match-play golfer Eric Brown, in their much-talked-of Ryder Cup eyeball-to-eyeball duel at Lindrick, which Brown won by 4 and 3. At a short hole during the afternoon round, Bolt hit an iron shot through the green, immediately blamed his caddie for over-clubbing him and, in a hot-blooded outburst, buried the head of the iron up to the shaft in the teeing-ground. So much thunderbolt passion was employed in this demonstration that the shaft vibrated and quivered like a tuning-fork. When he was forced to concede the match to Brown on the fifteenth green – after making a complete hash of that hole – he did so by swiping Brown's ball (which lay close to the hole in two) straight off the green!

However, the story I like best about Bolt is the one told by George Plimpton, author of *The Bogey Man*. It describes a conversation between Bolt and his caddie, as follows:

CADDIE: Mr Bolt, you'll be using either a 2- or a 3-iron for this shot.

BOLT (incredulously): Hell, man, that's 350 yards out there. Ol' Tom can't begin to reach the green with a 2-, much less a 3-iron.

CADDIE: Mr Bolt, all you got left in your bag are those two clubs. Unless you want to use your putter.

BOLT: Oh.

CADDIE: And your putter's missin' its handle. You snapped it off on the first nine.

BOLT: Oh.

If any golfer was in a wilderness of superiority, it was Bobby Locke, with his phenomenal putting, and perhaps even more so because he slept with his putter to safeguard against its being stolen. For the truth was that Bobby won so many tournaments in America, he thought someone might creep into his boudoir at the dead of night and, taking care not to trip over his immaculately cut knickers, appropriately hooked on the bedpost, dash off with his magic wand.

But JoAnne Carner, American star of the women's tour – whom everyone in the States affectionately calls 'Big Momma' – ended Locke's superiority in this respect. She once needed only 23 putts in a round (two fewer than her previous best) and was so delighted that she said: 'I don't want to tell my husband about this, but I must – I'm going to sleep with my putter tonight. He's going to have to sleep in the other bed!'

You're a pretty superior golfer if you've scored an albatross (a 3-under-par hole) at any time in your career on the links. But you're even more in a wilderness of superiority if you've bagged *two* of them, like the chap who wrote to the editor of a golf magazine to tell him so. However, in composing his letter, he ran into trouble with the correct plural, as follows: 'Dear Mr Editor, I should like you to know that in my golfing life I can boast of having scored two albatross.' He didn't like the look or the sound of that, and so tore up the letter and started again. 'Dear Mr Editor, I should like you to know that in my golfing life I can boast of having scored two albatrosses.' But this second version didn't satisfy him any more than the first, so he tore it up once more and wrote: 'Dear Mr Editor, I should like you to know that in my golfing life I can boast of having scored an albatross – and, by the way, I also had another.'

2 First Tee Phobia

My theme on this occasion is a real scary one – no less than first-tee phobia. But I propose including something to blunt the edge of it, something you're already doing, I trust, as you sit in your armchair. It is *breathing*. However, if, by some unfortunate mischance, you're not doing it, kindly read no further. For what I'm about to say of the art of breathing as related to the art of golfing will be of no immediate interest to you.

For everyone else, inhaling and exhaling nobly, I can promise a super tip from Tom Watson, five times Open champion, coupled with the illustrious name of Reginald Whitcombe, Open champion, 1938. But, for the moment, please be patient and try to remain composed until I can find time to return to these two fine golfers a little later on in the script …

A day or two ago, while out walking in town with an untroubled mind, I turned a corner and suddenly saw a placard outside a church. 'IF YOUR KNEES ARE KNOCKING,' it said, 'WHY NOT KNEEL ON THEM?'

Good, prayer-bone stuff – except for the bowlegged fraternity – but more than a little worrying for the golfer suffering from first-tee phobia. For, I ask you, is there anyone knocking around the universe whose knees knock more than his? They knock so much – especially on the first tee – that they knock the bottom out of his market. So how could he hope to overcome his nervousness by *kneeling*? Clever guys like Seve Ballesteros and Bobby Clampett drive while kneeling, it's true, but they kneel for kicks, not to stop their knees knocking.

Of all places on a golf course, the first tee is the one that strikes terror into a golfer's heart. No matter whether he's a professional or amateur, old hand or raw beginner, the first tee is the spot on the golfing map where control of the nervous system is most blessed of all. Indeed, I often think that the first tee is rather like the stage on an opening night. There's a

17

dramatic strung-up, breathless air about, and as the time for curtain-rise approaches, the players most affected by nerves are contemplating whether or not to go off and hang themselves. I recall an actress who was so nervous on opening night (and so full of gin) that it was all the rest of the company could do to stop her falling over the footlights and pitching head-first into the orchestra pit. A kindly critic wrote: 'She gave a simply staggering performance, but showed signs of not being fully recovered from a recent illness.' Pure eyewash, of course. As most theatre-goers knew, she hadn't had anything the matter with her for years.

First-tee phobia affects most golfers, particularly on the big occasion, and pro-am get-togethers are events where the nerve-ends protrude raggedly for most amateurs. Pro-Celebrity Golf on TV is always notable for the many celebrities who declare themselves to be nervous wrecks on the first tee. Being paired with the legendary Arnold Palmer or the evergreen Gary Player is enough to drive the wits – and hits – out of any golfer; and if you add the hassle of cameras and producers, well-wishers and spectators, you arrive at a situation guaranteed to make the amateur performer as desperate as if his mother-in-law was visiting him next week.

Patrick Campbell told a funny story of a golfer in a pro-am event who was so nervous that he fell over in the simple act of teeing his ball, and the handle of his driver shot up the sleeve of his jersey and emerged at the shoulder. Although incapacitated in this way, he managed to stand up, but neither he nor his caddie could get the driver down again, and the pro's caddie had to lend a hand. Hours seemed to go by. At a second shot at driving off, the fellow struck the ladies' tee-box and rebounded under a seat.

One of Patrick's own pro-am, first-tee experiences, while partnering a distinguished professional, was even more outside the laws of probability. With a wild, boomerang drive, he hit a double-decker bus in the car-park and woke the bus-driver who had been asleep inside. Declaring his ball unplayable, Campbell drove again, reached the green in one over par, but then played much too strongly and hit his professional partner (who was lighting a cigarette at the time) on the ankle. Asked if he remembered the pro's name, Campbell discreetly said he didn't.

Which was just as well, for he recalled that the pro took three putts from two yards.

All golfers will hope to avoid incidents of this nature, but how are they to quieten their nerves long enough to drive a decent ball? The answer – as Sherlock Holmes would have said – is elementary, according to Tom Watson.

'You often see pressure in pro-ams,' says Tom, 'especially at the first tee; it blocks many amateurs from doing their best. I try to help by saying I usually am nervous, too.'

When asked what he thought the cure was, Tom replied: 'Breathing. Pressure tends to impair normal relaxed breathing. Deep breaths help. Sometimes good players may appear to be yawning on the course; in reality, they're probably trying to take deep breaths.'

Reginald Whitcombe, the golfer who, at the age of forty, won the 1938 Open by mastering a tremendous gale at Sandwich, was a great advocate of deep breathing on the links. Indeed, he began an instructional book on golf with a chapter entitled 'Breathe your way to scratch'. That's how important he felt good breathing to be. He advised the golfer to do breathing exercises in bed, in the bath, in an office or an armchair, or driving the car or playing the nineteenth hole.

'Don't hang out of your bathroom window on a winter morning and fill your lungs with frosty air,' said Whitcombe. 'Do it in the comfort of your bedroom. Do it in the warmth of your bathroom. Do it as you sit in state at your office. Do it in the car on the way to the links. Do it on the way to the tee. Do it as you walk after the ball. Do it while you wait for your opponent to putt. Don't wait until you have played your shot. Do your sighing first. Sigh first and hit after.'

Whitcombe said that controlled breathing meant control of yourself, of your nerves and of your golf.

So the next time you stand on the first tee with your knees getting far too intimate with one another, remember Whitcombe and Watson. After all, you don't want the shaft of your driver up the sleeve of your jersey or down the leg of your trousers, do you? Nor do you want even more calamitous things to happen, as the following story illustrates.

A TV producer, watching a pro-am at the first tee, saw a professional executing fantastic hand-springs and incredible somersaults. He stood amazed, and presently said to one of the golfers: 'What an acrobat! Do you think he'd sign up for a TV spectacular?'

'He might,' replied the golfer,'but you'd have to engage Alf as well.'

'Who's Alf?' asked the producer.

'The amateur bloke wot 'it him with his driver!' said the golfer.

3   A Paradoxical Game

A golfer playing alone on the links is not unlike T.S. Eliot's mystery cat, Macavity. So far as the law is concerned, neither he nor Macavity is actually there. Of course, the law – in the golfing context – isn't Scotland Yard, as with Macavity, but the Royal and Ancient and the Rules of Golf, for a single player has no standing and, paradoxically, isn't there at all.

Perhaps it's a pity that the lone golfer isn't recognized on the links. Playing alone can be far more agreeable than playing with some Clever Dick who is everlastingly telling you what you're doing wrong or saying how marvellously he played a week last Tuesday or once got an eagle by holing a 3-iron from a bad lie.

'It's astounding how many boring, irrelevant details a golfer can remember of his last round,' said a sufferer recently, 'and I've come to the conclusion that one should never make the mistake of asking how a golfer played, particularly if he talks of having played well.' He added, rather severely I thought, that the most attractive thing about any golfing companion is, as Sydney Smith said of Macaulay, the occasional flashes of silence that make his conversation perfectly delightful.

Apart from the more obvious paradoxes of golf, like hitting *down* to make the ball fly *up*, swinging *right* to make it fly *left* and *left* to fly it *right*, one of the game's truest paradoxes is that it is the best game at which to be bad. Viscount Grey, briefly mentioning golf in his *Fallodon Papers*, said: 'Anyone can be taught the rules of the game and how to play golf. One person may turn out to be a very good player and another an indifferent player, yet even an indifferent player may find so much pleasure in the game that it becomes an enthusiasm and a passion.'

Anyone who has played for any length of time knows this to be so. The lousy golfer is the one who gets all the fun and, unlike other sports, he's always sure of getting his fair share of the game. Even more than his share, if he knocks up a cricketing

score every time out, with more sixes than even Ian Botham dreams of. Contrast his share of the game with that of the mediocre cricketer who – stumps spreadeagled first ball – is no sooner strapped into his pads than out of them again, and we can see why the analysts declare golf a good game at which to be bad.

What is more, the occasional good stroke of the bad golfer is a joy forever, whereas the occasional bad stroke of the good golfer makes him so suicidal that he can hardly wait to get home to stick his head in the gas-oven. On second thoughts, perhaps a microwave oven would be kinder to him, as it would put an end to his miseries so much more quickly. At any rate, it's clear that just one or two good shots in a round are all the bad player asks of golf, while the good player who hits a single bad shot is like someone riding a solid-tyre bike over cobbles – he feels the experience painfully beneath him all the time!

For the tournament giants, who normally score only in par or under-par figures, golf can be perversely paradoxical. Without warning, seemingly absurd scores may pop up to register double figures on the card. The great man, Arnold Palmer, needing a par 5 for a 69 in the 1961 Los Angeles Open, finished with a 12. When someone asked him to explain his lapse, he said: 'I missed the putt for an 11.' Golfers who bore us stiff by describing how they played certain holes should note this classic comment of Palmer's. Short and to the point, with a nice touch of irony.

Tom Weiskopf, playing Augusta's twelfth hole – a mere 155-yarder – in the 1980 Masters, put his tee shot into the water alongside the green. This is a common enough error at Augusta, for the 12th is a particularly testing tee-shot, and the loss of one or two strokes is the usual outcome. But Weiskopf pitched four more balls into the water and finally holed-out in 13.

More recently, in the 1984 Open at St Andrews, the Open winner at Sandwich in 1981, Bill Rogers, ran up a 12 at the par 5 14th – quite an asburdity for a former champion's card. He finished the round in 82, which was splendid, but golf's capriciousness had created another paradoxical sensation.

Great golfers are a bit like the performing flea that fired a cannon but never got accustomed to its role in life – for the flea was said to be no less dismayed and confounded by the thousandth report than by the first. The flea shocked by its own cannon-fire is similar to the first-class golfer scandalized by a double-figure hole on his card.

The essayist G.K. Chesterton rarely wrote on golf, but whenever he put pen to paper there was sure to be a paradox or two involved. He wrote an amusing piece entitled *On Aids to Golf* in which he quoted a philosopher (whose name he had forgotten!) who said: 'The Charleston may be of great practical use in teaching a man to be a good golfer.' However, Chesterton didn't agree. He thought the statement would be better the other way round: 'Golf may really be of great practical use in teaching us to dance the Charleston.' His explanation was simple. He said it was unreasonable for a man to dance with a girl in order to play golf. Moreover, the idea of a golfer suddenly leaving off dancing because he thought he'd danced the Charleston long enough to reduce his handicap, or explaining to a girl that he was only dancing with her for the good of his golf, offended Chesterton. 'It would be almost better to rush madly away without any explanation at all,' he said, 'to leap wildly through the window in the direction of the links.'

Chesterton once declared: 'The men who really believe in themselves are all in lunatic asylums.' What he didn't tell us was how many of them were golfers ...

4 Come on in, the Water's Fine

'I must say, Mrs Nicklaus,' said the clergyman genially, 'I've never christened such a well-behaved baby as Jack.'

'Ah, well, you see,' said Mrs Nicklaus, 'we've been getting him used to it with a watering-can.'

This little story – a watery lie – is apocryphal, of course, but it serves admirably as an introduction to the remarkable flair that Jack Nicklaus has for playing shots out of watery lies – shots which most other golfers, professional or amateur, wouldn't think of attempting.

Being called upon to knock the ball across a stretch of water makes most handicap golfers 'quake like a jelly in a high wind'. It also raises an air of expectancy in their opponents and onlookers, who stand about with disconcerting smirks on cynical faces, just waiting for the awful *plop* and resultant splash. Yet these are the shots – even where the carry is inordinately long – that seem so easy to the professionals and low-figure players, though occasionally even *they* meet with disaster and find themselves trapped in the stuff.

Playing in the Doral Eastern Open in Miami, Nicklaus hooked a 4-iron into the big lake by the eighteenth green and, rather than pick out and drop, chose to remove his shoes and socks in an adventurous paddle. Some minutes later, the gallery was roaring its approval as Jack's resourcefulness and wedge splashed the ball out of the shallow water to within some twelve feet of the hole.

'I'd made a previous par 4 from roughly the same spot, so I figured I might do the same again,' said Jack, as he gave his summing-up later. Although he narrowly missed the putt and had to be content with a bogey 5, his remarkable expertise at playing from water had been demonstrated once again.

I recall a similar water-shot of pure delight that Nicklaus played at Augusta in the 1979 Masters, when his ball pitched on the bank at the fifteenth green and trickled tantalizingly back into the water.

Fisherman Jack circled the pond and weighed the possibilities. His ball was lying in only a couple of inches of water, so there was a chance of splashing out. On went his waterproof jacket. Up went his pants, rolled to the knee. Down into the pond he stepped. A careful look, an iron's sudden flash and splash, and there the ball lay, ten feet from the stick. It had leapt out like a Nicklaus-struck fish, obedient to the Master's art.

Jacket off, pants rolled down, a quick shake, like a big water-loving dog (or should I say *bear*?) and there was Jack striding purposefully across the green to knock in the tiddler, after the usual hypnotic meditation.

Now, there are those who declare that there's no way in which you can practise water shots. But for golfers who don't mind getting wet and perhaps a little muddy, Nicklaus tells us that playing out of *shallow* water is much like blasting from a buried lie in sand. If the ball rests just below the water's surface (say two inches), it can be played successfully. He says: 'The idea is to sort of *cut* the ball out. So address the shot with an open clubface and open stance, then pick the club up abruptly on the backswing. Hit down sharply and try to catch as much of the ball as possible. Let the clubhead go deep into the mud or sand after impact.'

Not a shot for the squeamish, of course, but easy meat for anyone coached in infancy with a watering-can. But Nicklaus is so good at these watery lies, one wonders if those fishing trips are a means to an end. Does he take a wedge with him and practise recoveries from the river's edge?

If you should decide to splash your way out of water, in either play or practice, take care not to lose your balance and sit down in the stuff. It could be a dampening experience, as a lady golfer found to her dismay at Ilkley, Yorkshire, on the River Wharfe. Playing a hole alongside the flooded river, she overbalanced, fell backwards and suddenly found herself having to swim for it. Her caddie – obviously a gentleman of initiative and promptitude – thrust out a club for her to grasp and pull herself out. Doubtless one of the rare occasions when there was no great argument about club-selection, which was left entirely to him ...

Not only was the lady a strong swimmer, she was a strong

personality on the course, too, for when she came out and shook the water from her ears, she continued to play the hole – which she eventually won!

A married couple once took off their shoes and socks on the Moretonhampstead course, high up on the shoulder of Dartmoor, on an oppressively hot afternoon in 1976, a summer of endless sunshine and high temperatures. The husband had put his ball into the River Bovey and removed his shoes and socks to try to play out of the shallows. But, having stepped down into the stream, he found the water so exquisitely cool and refreshing to his burning hot feet that he didn't want to come out.

'Come on in!' he shouted to his wife. 'The water's fine – it's lovely and cool.'

And she, being quite unable to resist the thought of paddling in a cool Dartmoor stream, quickly joined him. Her feet were on fire, anyway, and that was good enough reason to risk whatever malicious scandal might result from adjourning the round for half-an-hour's paddling.

So there was quite a gulf between the intention and the result, and I never did learn whether the fellow attempted the watery lie. All I know is that golfers, coming hot-foot behind them, were delighted to be waved through and not at all curious about the couple and their frivolous mood. I guess they thought they were recovering a ball, not tickling trout or merely cooling hot feet.

Finally, just to prove that not all golfers are afraid of water, there's the story of the teetotal Rear-Admiral who was lunching at a golf club where abstainers were not the general rule.

He called the waiter and said impatiently: 'I've asked you five times to bring me a glass of water.'

'Yes, I know, sir,' replied the waiter, 'and the staff's had a jolly good laugh. But don't carry the joke too far.'

5 Strictly on the Quiet

There once was a golfer who used to win his matches by making a study beforehand of his opponent's pet hates and then talking about them in a provocative manner during the round. For example, by goading his adversary with a running conversation on the possibilities of life on Mars, he reached the final of the Captain's Prize; and the President's Bowl came to him as a result of a carefully-thought-out, antagonistic condemnation of the eight-ball over.

Of course, tiring the sun with talking and sending him down the sky in a four- or five-hour round of golf is a commonplace performance of golfers the world over and, quite apart from whether or not they talk to win matches, raises the question: 'Do present-day golfers talk too much?'

Such a question seems relevant to a statement in a recent issue of an American golf magazine, in which Lee Trevino is reported to have said that Fuzzy Zoeller should donate his body to medical science. 'His mouth is worn out but his ears are brand new,' said Trevino.

Like me, I dare say you'll feel somewhat mystified over this remark, but we can only assume that Lee thinks Fuzzy talks too much and listens too little. However, since the ebullient Super-Mex suffers from the same occupational hazard, we may conclude that (as a sardonic host said of a particularly talkative husband and wife) when one tongue stops, the other starts.

Chatty, out-going, happy-go-lucky characters such as Trevino and Zoeller are very different from golfers who prefer to talk as little as possible during play, the latter holding the view that extraneous talk sometimes gums up one's golf.

Ben Hogan preferred not to talk during a round. He once met Jimmy Demaret over thirty-six holes of matchplay and defeated him by 10 and 9. When Demaret was asked what the turning-point of the match was, he replied: 'The first tee this morning.' He was then asked if Hogan had much to say. No.

Occasionally he spoke a couple of words on the green. What were they? 'You're away,' answered Demaret.

All said in the very best of humour, I'm sure, for Demaret was the nicest of fellows and a popular wit on and off the course. As a great golfer, he was the first to win three Masters Tournaments, doubtless by chatting his way all through them.

Golfers who are put off by talk seem rare as re-paints these days. I suspect that sensitive players who sought refuge in ear-plugs and cottonwool (and even zipper-mouthed guys who growled: 'Let's cut the cackle and get on with it!') are by this time resting under large divots, well out of ear-shot, with a bowl of forget-me-nots holding them down. But, if you were able to question them, they would tell you that their ear-plugs and cottonwool were a complete failure. No less an authority than Henry Cotton tried them, but found it almost impossible to judge a shot without being able to hear the impact and click of the ball.

Deaf golfers who believe in quietly concentrating on the game may be on to something good. Like a singed cat, their deficiency may be better than it looks. If they turn a deaf ear to their opponents, with their hearing-aid prominently displayed, they need only remove it to ensure absolute silence for the remainder of the round.

Arnold Palmer, now slightly deaf in the right ear, is going to the opposite extreme by choosing to wear a hearing-aid on what is termed 'an experimental basis'. 'Arnie has admitted that he has a slight hearing problem,' says Doc Giffin, Palmer's long-time associate, 'but right now he doesn't know if he'll use an aid all the time.' This pronouncement leaves Arnie free to listen or turn a deaf ear, simply by wearing or removing the aid.

Just how narrow is the divide which separates the advantages of golfing with or without conversation may soon be discovered by a careful monitoring (if that's the right word!) of Palmer's future form. Perhaps some eagle-eyed statistician will compile tables of Fairways Hit, Greens in Regulation, Sand Saves and so on, under separate headings of 'With Hearing-Aid' and 'Without Hearing-Aid'. We may then know if our own performance on the links could be bettered by telling everyone politely to shut up.

Edison, the great inventor, was slightly deaf, but was never heard to deplore his deafness. Indeed, he often spoke of it as beneficial. He said it helped him to concentrate upon the problems he was trying to solve. A friend once asked him if he had lost anything by his deafness. 'No, nothing important,' he replied. 'Most of the conversation in which the public engages is only chaff. By being deaf, I am spared all this chaff and I have a better chance to get my work done.'

Edison, as a golfer, might have been able to tell us if golfers lose anything by having to listen to an opponent blether on about the secret ingredients of crab-apple jelly, but my computer has failed to reveal the inventor's golf club, handicap or even passing interest in the game.

As a young politician, Winston Churchill declared golf to be a good game for conversation, but in later years gave up the game and wore a hearing-aid with distinction. Had Winnie's interest in golf continued, he might have contributed a few well-chosen words on golfing gasbags: 'Give us the cottonwool, and we will finish the round.'

In the House of Commons, Churchill used to confound speakers by the simple expedient of noticeably removing his hearing-aid and placing it conspicuously on the bench in front of him. By this action, he was able silently to indicate his disagreement or boredom with what was being said. On second thoughts, perhaps the assumption was incorrect. I guess it could have been that his batteries had suddenly gone flat.

Ploys of a similar nature could be used to our advantage if we were pitted against the type of opponent who – as Stephen Potter said – 'plays every course as if it were a public meeting and makes shouting conversation with embarrassed acquaintances on the next fairway.' Also, in much the same way as Potter's eccentric spectator used to walk the links with a cardboard walkie-talkie on his back as a manoeuvre for stepping through big crowds and getting the best view of play, we could sport a false hearing-aid for the first hole or two and, on removing it, ensure silence for the rest of the round.

It used to be said that many of the old-time professionals played their best golf by favouring the shut face and low-flying ball, to which it could be added that many amateurs produced their worst golf as a result of an opponent's open face – particularly in the area between the ears, above the chin and directly beneath the nose!

'I cannot see the wit of walking and talking at the same time,' said William Hazlitt. The only exception he was prepared to make was to talk of what there would be at the evening's inn for supper. Thought of eggs and a rasher of bacon or a rabbit smothered in onions would break his silence.

Lastly, by an extraordinary coincidence, comes the story of an American golfer declaring that an Englishman with whom he travelled to Edinburgh for the Open at St Andrews spoke only two words during the entire journey. Asked what he thought of this, an Irish golfer said: 'Be gob, there must have been a moighty good rayson for disturbin' the feller wid sitch an outburst!'

6   Stimpmeters on the Carpet

I talked recently with a golfing farmer who was enthusiastic over his new-found putting technique.

'My putting had been so *bad*, so unbelievably *rotten*,that I decided to work it out for myself on the carpet at home and, much to my wife's disgust, spent three hours at it without a break, rolling one putt after another between a couple of books balanced on end, with another book as backstop.'

'What length of carpet have you to practise on?' asked a long-faced fellow who, only that morning, had three-putted five times within twenty feet.

'About eighteen feet,' said the farmer. 'But my carpet not only has a decent length for practice, it also has the distinct advantage of being laid on top of an undulating floor. Putts not only move appreciably from side to side but have to be hit uphill and downhill as well. That's the beauty of living in a seventeenth-century farmhouse. The floor allows you to borrow a bit and also teaches you to lag up where it hurries downhill.'

'Does this mean that we should all rush out and buy old farmhouses with long, uneven floors in order to become expert putters?' I asked. 'My usual vice of buying and discarding a succession of putters seems inexpensive by comparison.'

'It isn't the floor. It isn't the carpet. And it isn't the putter,' answered the farmer. 'It's the technique. I've worked out a marvellous method of hitting my putts exactly half-way between the centre and toe of the putter-blade. And it's *incredible*. The ball goes into the middle of the hole every time. I feel I can't miss.'

'Bobby Locke advocates addressing the ball with the toe of the putter, but actually striking it with the centre of the blade,' said a listener, whose chief claim to fame was that he had once stood alongside Locke in the gents at Moor Park.

'Did Bobby mention, when you stood alongside him in the

gents at Moor Park, whether he practised on carpets in South African farmhouses with dodgy, undulating floors?' asked a mocking fellow.

'Talking of putting on the carpet,' said another golfer. 'I heard of a chap who always went to the same hotel and insisted on having the same bedroom because the carpet there was just the right speed for practising putting.'

'What did he do?' asked a sceptical voice. 'Test it with a Stimpmeter?'

'Ben Hogan always appreciated a hotel carpet of the right speed,' observed a rather shaky gin-and-tonic. 'I'll bet he would have carried a Stimpmeter in his suitcase, if they'd been in vogue in his day.'

'Ben was thoroughness itself,' I said. 'You'd probably find he had the hotel staff cut new holes in the carpet every night.'

Discussion then centred on professional golfers practising their putting strokes in hotel bedrooms throughout the world. Our assembly fell to wondering if the pros had idiosyncratic views on the speed of bedroom carpets, fast and slow, average distance of roll, and so on. One guy wondered if the pros were extremely annoyed when they got a hotel carpet totally unsuited to putting. What if they got well and truly lumbered with a fluffy pile suitable only for chipping?

But the golfer who had spoken earlier of the man who always booked at the same hotel, requesting the same bedroom because of carpet-speed, said that the chap arrived on one occasion to find that the hotel was under new management and all the bedrooms re-carpeted with a pile so deep that you could actually *lose* a golf ball in it!

Well, that about wrapped up our analysis of the subject, but I was reminded of George Plimpton's humorous description of reserving a room at a San Francisco hotel, with a view to practising his putting on the carpet previous to competing as an amateur in the Lucky International.

He asked for a *large* room, 'something in the forty-foot-by-forty-foot bracket', but finally chose a suite because the room was even larger and would provide him with the opportunity of practising long approach putts.

Having had the desk clerk's assurances that the room wasn't L-shaped, Plimpton was taken to the suite by a bellboy, riding up in the elevator to the fourth floor, to find the room enormous and ideally suited to rolling up long putts. But then he noticed that the floor was not laid with carpet throughout, but merely scattered about with small rugs on a polished parquet surface!

Plimpton's subsequent efforts to explain to the hotel staff that he was scheduled to play in a golf tournament on the following day and wanted a room where he could practise putting (and now wished to change his suite for a large room with wall-to-wall carpeting) were never clearly and sympathetically understood, and the misunderstanding got so out of hand that one of the suite's rugs was taken away for cleaning.

However, as addicts of the little white ball know only too well, it's no uncommon thing for a golfer's schemes to go unexpectedly wrong, no matter how well planned or carefully thought out they may be, and the furtive fellow who insists on accompanying his wife to the furniture store on the pretext of helping her choose new carpets (albeit with a Stimpmeter concealed in his dispatch case) may find himself in difficulties over colour schemes, designs and the absurd emphasis placed on matching carpets with curtains. Unless he's of exceptional personality and strength of character (what's known in farmyard parlance as a 'chauvinistic pig'), his wife may tell him – even in front of the carpet salesman – what he can do with his Stimpmeter. In short, he'll be jolly lucky if he manages to get it out of his dispatch case, let alone test the speed of carpets. Still, if there's a golfer who manages to do so, I shall be glad to hear about it – as the deaf man said to his ear-trumpet.

Perhaps, as in reeling off par figures, it's simply a matter of starting as you mean to go on, like the man who combined a golfing holiday with his honeymoon. He received his bride, stunningly attired in a sensational nightdress, in their hotel bedroom and, with perfectly good manners and loving forethought, said: 'And now what would you like to do, darling? I'm all for testing the speed of this carpet with my Stimpmeter.'

7 The Links of Don Quixote

– or A Parody of Mental Imagery

Light of heart, Don Quixote issued forth from the clubhouse soon after break of day, his spiked shoes flashing in the bright morning sunlight. In lieu of a Lee Trevino cap or a Ken Brown knitted tea-cosy, a barber's basin was on his head, glittering as though made of gold.

A line of golf-carts stood waiting, but Don Quixote saddled Rosinante, fastened his bag of golf clubs across the steed's neck and mounted him with a typical flourish. Whilst Rosinante was available, he had no intention of using a trolley and, giving the beast a deft flick with his Nicklaus spikes, the two of them set off at a gallop towards the seventh hole.

A man who could tilt at windmills believing them to be giants with long arms, could easily master the striking of a little white ball, and Don Quixote, strong on mental imagery, was eager for the combat.

'Golf,' he said to Rosinante as they jogged along, 'is merely the art of picturing a shot and then playing it, instead of playing without a thought and then having to go off and fish the ball out of a lake. It is the calm assumption that you have the mastery to dispatch your ball to a predetermined spot, rather than being, so to speak, unable to hit a bull with a shovel.'

According to the Don's latest golf book, all he had to do was form a clear, imaginary picture of the ball sitting on the green, a yard from the flagstick.

Only the previous evening, he had seen a number of golfers coming in on the homeward half. And, by Sancho Panza!, a more unhappy bunch of assassins he'd yet to see.

Some were pushing. Others were pulling. Some were slicing. Others were hooking. A few were socketing. At least one was frothing at the mouth. An old chap, up to his ears in rough, appeared to be beating something to death with his wedge.

It was enough to make even the stoutest-hearted knight-errant feel nervous, and – of course – perfectly obvious that none of these players knew anything of mental imagery.

That same evening at the short 7th, he had stood watching a couple of golfers. One appeared to be a reasonably good player, but there was a tendency to hurry the downswing, as though he were attempting to behead an adder. The fellow's partner was even worse. He sent two balls into the pond and three into the wood, and then went off muttering to himself, like a Spaniard whose onions have come unstrung.

Don Quixote had to smile to himself as he watched them, for he knew quite well where they had gone wrong. It was as plain as fish to a cat and could be summed up in two words: *Mental* and *Imagery*.

Don Quixote pulled Rosinante to a halt at the seventh hole, where it was his intention to practise. Removing his sword, he poured a liberal supply of practice balls at his feet and, taking a Harry Vardon grip on a 4-iron, unleashed a few practice swings.

Then, opening up his shooting-stick, he sat down and, putting on his reading glasses – and slipping Rosinante a few sugar-lumps, became engrossed in his golf book and the chapter on mental imagery. Before hitting a single ball, the Don intended to make sure everything was right.

As he read, he was glad to confirm that, if he formed a clear mental image of the ball resting on the green, all would be well.

Apparently, it had something to do with the subconscious taking over and playing the shot for you. Which, as he confided to Rosinante, was pretty decent of the subconscious.

Don Quixote closed the book and selected a ball. Teeing it up carefully, he imagined it to be flying straight for the green and – getting perfect reception – saw it pitch and roll into the hole. *O Dulcinea, my princess! Magnificent!*

Now for the actual shot. Taking his stance, he whipped his 4-iron at the ball and, lifting his head to observe the result, was just in time to see a flash of white diving into the undergrowth.

Undaunted (as befits a knight-errant) he teed another ball, thought of the same green, got the same picture, watched his ball slip into the cup – and swung his iron.

This time, as he looked up, the green was in his sights, but there was no ball preparing to drop on it.

Suddenly, out of the furthermost corner of his eye, he caught sight of something sneaking off towards the wood.

And then Don Quixote heard noises which he diagnosed as (1) a golf ball outside a wood trying to get in and (2) a golf ball inside a wood trying to get out.

When all this beating about had died down, he teed another ball and, though he said it himself, hit a really powerful shot.

Unfortunately, hitting a tree trunk fair and square, it came zooming back like a boomerang and hit Rosinante behind the ear.

He teed another ball.

He teed another sixteen balls.

And then a splendid idea came to Don Quixote. As he bent down for another ball, he saw the golf book and his shooting-stick resting side by side on the turf. *He thought of a new way of dealing with mental imagery.*

With his eyes bulging from their sockets and his teeth bared in a vicious snarl, he seized his shooting-stick and, raising its wicked-looking point above his head, he teed the book.

And – just to make doubly sure – he then ran it through with his sword.

8 The Virtues of One-Club Golf

Bernard Darwin, perhaps the greatest golf-writer the game has ever known, was much addicted to one-club golf. He called it 'that heavenly pottering with one club'. Throughout his golfing life, he enjoyed nothing better than being alone with a single club and a ball. Give him some out-of-the-way spot on the links (or even a meadow behind the house) and he was at his happiest. Not for him the common practice ground where the caddie retrieved the balls. He preferred some lone valley on the links where the kindly sandhills hid him from prying eyes. Although by no means an unfriendly or uncompanionable man, he thought the solitariness of pottering over the links with a club and a ball a great joy. 'How can we run and sing with joy over a great shot with even the smallest boy to goggle at us?'

Darwin used to take his club and a few balls to the seashore at St Andrews. 'The only place in that crowded kingdom of men where one may sometimes hope for the absence of one's fellow men.' Swinging his solitary club there on the wet sand was described as thrilling.

There were many favourite courses and fields where Darwin was happy to wander about with one club. He liked Hoylake's flat landscape, particularly in the quiet of the evening. 'I remember happy wanderings over it in the dusk, till the lights came out one by one in the surrounding houses, and I could only see, dimly looming, the shapes of the bunkers.'

In my mind's eye, I see Darwin as a pale shadow against the Hoylake skyline. A phantom golfer, wandering the links where the local-born John Ball and Harold Hilton wandered before him, gracefully hitting a ball here and there till the tired sun faded out. Perhaps, like his much-cherished Sam Weller, he whistled cheerfully as he went along, 'several of the most popular airs of the day, as arranged with entirely new movements for that noble instrument the organ, either mouth or barrel'.

Not unlike Sir Walter Simpson's shepherd tending his sheep, coming upon a round pebble and, having a crook in his hand, striking it away. A man with a crook or stick in his hand is very akin to the one-club golfer. But pottering about on the links with one club is a greatly neglected part of the golf scene these sophisticated days. One might almost say that the golfer who does it is something of an eccentric. Yet it's pleasing to know that one of the leading players of the day, Seve Ballesteros, and one of the leading theorists and teachers, John Jacobs, began the game with one club, as caddies, and each is now extolling the virtues of one-club golf on course or practice ground.

Ballesteros attributes his ability to play great recovery shots from almost impossible places to the fact that, in his young and formative days as a caddie, he had to learn to play all kinds of shots with a 5-iron. With that one club he chipped, hooked, faded, splashed out of bunkers and also putted! Seve believes that all handicap golfers could improve their game if they practised with only one iron, finding out for themselves the different ways of flighting the ball, together with the ingenuities of basic shot-invention.

John Jacobs, one of the most respected coaches in the game today, has recently been saying much the same as Ballesteros. He too began as a caddie and became adept at flighting the ball to varying heights and distances with a single straight-faced club. As a caddie with other boys at Lindrick, he used to wager tee-pegs on these one-club subtleties.

A good round of golf with only one club is by no means impossible. One-club competitions are a lot of fun, too, and, in taking part in them, handicap golfers can learn a great deal. Having to play all the shots with the same club breeds a confidence to invent and produce any kind of shot. Putting may be a little difficult at first, of course, but – like riding a camel or playing the tuba – you can get used to anything. For some years, Joe Carr, former Amateur Champion, Irish International and Walker Cup player, chose to putt with a 3-iron rather than use a putter.

Scores in the low 70s with one club are quite commonplace by good handicap golfers. If a player takes the care to stay out of trouble and play safely, really impressive figures may come his way. Besides, the short game shows up in a better light when the approach shots are played with a straight-faced club instead of one with loft. The sharpest of golfers can muff a chip with a 7-, 8- or 9-iron, but he rarely does so with a straight-faced club.

Perhaps the biggest advantage of one-club golf is the speed of play; for, whereas it takes three or four hours or longer to play a round with fourteen clubs, golf-trolley, golfbag as big as a performing seal, and all the rest of the paraphernalia, with only one club it's possible to get round in an hour and a half to two hours, without hurrying in the slightest. What's more, there's a delightfully unrestricted feeling about it. Just strolling along with one hand in your pocket and a golf-club-cum-walking stick in the other.

9 Mainly on One Leg

In America today, on practice grounds and in quiet corners of the links, there are thousands of golfers standing on one leg. Like a praying mantis or Long John Silver without his crutch, they stand, going through a one-legged drill towards striking a better golfing balance. Mostly they stand on the left leg, but – as any well-balanced Irishman will tell you – if they're lefties, you'll find them on the right!

Why are these golfers displaying such strange characteristics? Are they suffering from painful bunions or in-growing toenails? Are they performing some beneficial exercise from yoga? Or are they merely absent-minded, having put on someone else's shoes, two sizes too small, before leaving the locker-room?

None of these suggestions provides the answer. It is simply that Bob Toski, one of the leading teaching professionals in the States, is recommending his pupils to stand on one leg as a means of slowing down the tempo of the swing and improving golf balance. 'Standing on one leg helps the player who doesn't transfer his weight properly. The left leg should act as the support for the forward swing, so this drill is forcing you to do what you should do anyway. It teaches the feeling of hitting against and around the left side.'

Now, as David Attenborough's flamingos will confirm, standing on one leg isn't anything new. Indeed, it's been recommended in the past by many famous instructors, who readily demonstrated the idea, preferably in their more sober moments.

Ernest Jones, who had a leg amputated in the First World War and later became a highly-thought-of teaching professional in the States, said it was possible to swing a club from almost any position if the balance was maintained. 'I can sit in a chair and drive a ball 200 yards, and I frequently use this simple device to prove to pupils that, whereas there is one simple and

41

comfortable way to stand to the ball, there are many ways that one may swing.' Jones reminded us that trick-shot golfers entertained their galleries by hitting the ball from different stances and positions. One of these supernatural performers, the late Paul Hahn, used to stand on one leg on a seat-stick and whack the ball away from a high tee. Of course, his trick was made possible only because he kept a perfect balance as he swung.

Another American professional who believed that the secret of the swing lay in perfect balance was Eddie Loos. He also stood on one leg, and tried to take *full* swings whilst doing so. 'I made a discovery – a big one. Just so long as I let the club swing me, I hit the ball and was in perfect balance without thinking about it. The moment I tried to force the action of swinging the club, I couldn't keep in balance. That is all there is to it – let the club swing you – that's the feeling at any rate.'

Those American golfers who aren't philosophically swinging on one leg are lurking in quiet corners of the links *down on their knees*. You might think, if you saw them, they were praying for deliverance from weird hooks and slices, or maybe something equally bitter, like socketing or the putting yips. But you would be wrong. They're Bobby Clampett fans, proving to themselves that leg-action is of secondary importance in the golf swing. For Bobby says: 'I used to listen to teaching professionals say that power is generated by leg-action. And then I'd ask how come I could hit 210 yards off my knees.'

Clampett amused galleries in the 1979 US Open when, as a non-competing substitute in the last round, he hit drives on his knees, much to the chagrin of the USGA, who requested him to leave the course. But this exceptionally talented, ambidextrous young man finds his dramatic, on-the-knees shot very useful for recovering from under low-hanging trees. 'There's one other shot probably not too many people have seen,' he says. 'I can hit a left-handed drive on my knees about 190 yards using a right-handed driver.'

How would you like to try that remarkable shot? Most of us would wear out our kneecaps trying to perfect it!

Another remarkable indication of perfect golfing balance came recently from Sam Snead, whose doctor has said that nothing can be done about the deteriorating sight of his right eye. 'Every place I go, people tell me that the best eye doctor is in their town,' says Sam, now 71. 'All I know is that I can't see my drives land.' Whilst he was playing in a senior tournament recently, Sam's right eye swelled almost shut, and someone wanted to know how he could hit such great drives when he could barely see the ball.

'I can hit drives like that with *both* eyes shut,' said Sam.

Lack of balance can cause a great deal of trouble in golf – and not only in the *playing* of it. There's an old story to illustrate this.

A lady golfer, shocked at overhearing foul language used by men repairing overhead telephone lines at the clubhouse, sent a strongly worded complaint to the secretary. As a result, the foreman was asked to report on the incident, and his written statement read: 'I was up the pole and, suddenly losing my balance, let some hot lead fall upon Mike, my mate. Unfortunately, it went down his neck and he said: "You really must be more careful, Fred." '

10   Spiked Shoes in the Air

Golf Monthly's instruction columns are rightly regarded as great stuff. One glance at the impressive line-up of contributing professionals proves how comprehensively readers are catered for in their quest for the impeccably hit ball. So – if any reader buries his ball in the bracken off the first tee or carelessly thumps an onlooker behind the ear on the backswing – there's little point in asking for his money back; and it's no use saying (as one sly chap did), 'A bluebottle landed on my ball just as I was about to hit it!' – for as any contributing pro will tell you, balls sat on by passing bluebottles should be hit with rather more weight on the left foot and with an early straightening of the wrists just before impact.

Speaking of more weight on the left foot reminds me of comments from golfers who read my article 'Mainly On One Leg', advising them to swing on one leg as a means of improving balance. Quite a number were received, and it was sad to learn that one golfer, trying the tip for the first time, fell over suddenly and got mud on his trousers. Writing from Budleigh Salterton, he asked what I was going to do about it.

'My missis was furious,' he wrote. 'The trousers were a birthday present and cost the earth. I told her it was just mud and would brush off. But she said, "It's not *mud* – and doesn't smell like mud. It smells like something I'm not prepared to put a name to. It wouldn't be ladylike." I think she must have been referring to my driving out of bounds into a cow-pasture.'

Naturally enough, such comments seem preposterous to golfers who manage to balance easily on one leg, and I want to assure my readers that one-legged swinging can be carried out by beginners without the embarrassment of muddy trousers.

Let me give you my report.

After somewhat tentative beginnings and much wobbling about in the privacy of bedrooms and offices marked

'Conference – Do Not Disturb', one-legged swinging has become part of the daily golf curriculum on practice-grounds, tees, fairways and railway platforms. Of course, *Golf Monthly*'s ready endorsement of the idea quickly got spiked shoes off the ground. For example, only hours after publication, a London banker-cum-golfer's attempt to stand on one leg and essay a practice swing in Piccadilly circus resulted in his being escorted to a nearby police station. Questioned there on his Circus performance by the station sergeant, the banker explained that the idea was hot off the pages of *Golf Monthly*, and added that it was just as vital to strike the right balance in the game of golf as it was in the business of banking. Luckily the sergeant, being a keen golfer and regular reader of *Golf Monthly* (and an understanding and friendly officer to boot), agreed to further one-legged demonstrations being performed. As the magazine article passed from hand to hand, truncheons were swiftly drawn by all the golfing policemen present, and further experimental, one-legged swinging went on till well past midnight. In the course of these police investigations, it was found that policemen normally engaged on drink-drive offences toppled over less frequently than others and easily made the steadiest progress, their sense of balance being far superior to that of their colleagues.

Reports of one-legged swinging have come from all over Britain. For instance, a group of Liverpudlian golfers (said to be from Hoylake), having at length got the hang of swinging with spiked shoes off the ground, held a seminar alongside the seventeenth green. Balancing on one leg for several minutes at a time, they chatted with local residents passing along the road. Although it's understood that some northern banter occurred, the golfers refused to be put off balance, despite being told that they looked like a music-hall turn. No untoward incident occurred and no serious harm came to golfers frequently toppling over, though one senior golfer complained of muscular spasms and pins and needles, necessitating massage and a cold, well-loaded sponge slipped secretly down the back of his plus-twos. Recovering quickly, he nevertheless complained that the cure was disgustingly primitive and unscientific, like getting electricity out of a cat by stroking it the wrong way.

Perhaps the most unusual report came from London's musical life. A distinguished conductor – and enthusiastic amateur golfer – conducted Bruckner's Fifth Symphony while standing on one leg on the podium. He said: 'In Bruckner, as in the golf swing, it's important to interpret the tempi correctly. If the pauses do not fall precisely in place, you get the feeling that the score is coming apart.' He was given a standing ovation, during which it was noticed that quite a number of music-loving golfers stood on one leg as a mark of respect.

Meanwhile, like boys going downhill on a bicycle, the airborne feet of golfers have introduced a touch of comedy to greetings between members passing one another on the links. It's becoming a commonplace sight to see old golfers shaking a leg at one another instead of waving a hand or muddy towel.

There are a few – a very few – over-zealous reports of one-legged practice. Recently an acquaintance described to me rather shamefacedly how he thought that a Church of England vicar – whom he observed to be standing on one leg throughout his sermon – was improving his balance in preparation for golf. Chatted up at the conclusion of the service and asked where he played and what his handicap was, the vicar said that standing on one leg had nothing to do with golf. 'My handicap was simply a combination of new shoes and a distinctly nagging corn,' he declared, with a solemn and understandably painful grimace.

11   On the Identity Parade

Golf celebrities had come and gone. But now – as a Bobby Charlton pitch shot rose sharply from a lofted iron, to hover over the seventh green and then come down satisfyingly close to the flagstick, Ian Botham dropped in dramatically by helicopter alongside the eighteenth green.

The scene was the Exeter Golf and Country Club, and these two sportsmen (of large and small ball fame) – and many others – were in juxtaposition on the golf course, intent on doing their own thing with an even smaller ball and at the same time giving generously of their free time in aid of charity. On its best behaviour, a warm sun encouraged them to perform a shot or two above their best and, as Old Tom Morris always said, it was a grand morning for the game.

Spectators had already watched Henry Cooper, standing the wrong way round, crack a super drive up the first fairway. No need to ask who *he* was. Everyone knew 'Our 'Enery', and though he's a golfer of wide experience, he still looks something of an imposter, walking on tee or green as though entering the ring, giving the ball a hefty, homely punch, with occasional defiant uppercuts when he corners one in a bunker.

Of course, the autograph-hunters were everywhere on the identity parade, hounding Henry between holes, but he signed with immense patience, chatted with everyone, allowed TV interviews and camera sessions on the fairway and promised that Ian Botham – when his turn came – would captivate onlookers by hitting a long ball.

Meantime, Bobby Charlton – well into the outward half – was holding a sort of 'dressing-room pep-talk' with his amateur team, trying to inspire them to produce a few much-needed birdies. 'Come on, lads. We've turned the corner now. We can win this thing if we get stuck in!' But alas, as often happens to the unshakeable team-leader, Charlton climbed on to the tee and angled his drive into trees on the other fairway.

Mooching around the first tee, spectators watched other celebrities drive off. Ian Botham, not due to go off himself until after
lunch, was there, whiling away the time, chatting agreeably and
signing autographs for the never-ending knots of fans. Photographers milled around, clicking industriously at England's most
dynamic cricketer – the modern-day Jessop – and always asking
for more, like Oliver Twist.

Kenny Lynch, slim as a quartered pea-stick, was announced at
the tee as 'slightly sunburnt', paused in the act of teeing his ball
and waited for applause that didn't come.

'Well, come on, then, for Christ's sake!' he exclaimed, throwing
down his driver and clapping his hands in mock approval.

'Go ahead, Kenny. We'll give you a clap when we see what you
can do,' said critical-minded, mean-handed spectators.

He got his tee shot away nicely, though pushed out wide
towards rough on the right of the fairway. This is a common
direction of aim at Exeter, away from gardens flanking the left of
the fairway, landing-ground of many out-of-bounds first
attempts to a round.

A rush of autograph-hunters occurred as Eddie Large, curly-
headed comedian, entered the arena, complete with caddie and
huge 'Ping' bag, the repository of elegant equipment and
impressive black club-covers.

Someone whispered it around that Large is the Captain of the
Variety Club's Golf Association, and another onlooker asked:
'Where's your mate, Eddie?' – doubtless referring to Supersonic
Little, a non-golfer – and Eddie, bandying words with the jester's
touch, answered: 'He's in the boot of the car.'

The comedian's appearance sparked off another photographic
session, together with good-natured clowning and posing with
Botham.

'Hold the club like a cricket bat,' said the photographers to Ian.

'Get behind him and keep wicket,' Large was told.

And just when the pair were poised and ready for Take 64,
Botham gazed into the distance and expostulated: 'There's someone moving behind the bowler's arm!'

'Crouch down, Eddie. Look like you're going to stump him.'

'I *am* crouching! If I go down any further, I won't be able to get
up!'

Gradually the crowd at the first tee thickened, waiting for

Large to drive off. But he was in no hurry. With his wife alongside him, he nursed and cuddled their baby, Ryan, swinging him high in the air and down to the ground, in the relaxed, joyful way that proud fathers have. Viewed as a loosening-up exercise for a round of golf and an antidote against first-tee nerves, these baby-aerobatics seemed to set new pre-match standards by introducing a breezy, easy-going outlook that competing golfers normally don't have. One felt that, as a means of warming up for a round, baby-bouncing could be experimented with to good purpose, and possibly find its way into the textbooks. Certainly, in Large's sure hands, it looked the perfect method of relaxation and far better than the usual spell on practice-ground and putting-green.

However, when Large's turn came to drive off, even he saw the dangers on the left. 'A bit back-gardenish,' he declared, summing-up the tee-shot possibilities. But, like the trouper he is, he got away without disaster and the need to tee another ball.

Celebrities abounded. There was Brian This and Brian That – Close, Jacks, Godfrey and Rose – all signing the programmes of those who knew them, and often for those who didn't. Brian Jacks – of International Superstars fame – played all the way round with trousers tucked inside socks, and was spotted mishitting a tee shot a mere fifteen yards onto an adjacent green. Roars of laughter and shouts of 'Putt for a 2!' greeted his effort. Yet did it not emphasize the inherent difficulties of golf compared with all those other sports at which Jacks excels?

An isolated spectator in motorcycle gear stood in the middle of a fairway, cradling his crash-helmet as if it were a loaded goldfish bowl. What did they mean, shouting 'Four!' at him? Was he the fourth to get in their way? If so, where were 'One', 'Two' and 'Three'? He swept away humbly, walking backwards hurriedly and almost falling over, as golfers gesticulated and waved wildly from the tee.

A St John First Aid man, collecting autographs from every celebrity in sight, was asked if he'd had many casualties. No. Very quiet. No one dragged unconscious from the fairway, spouting blood from the head, he said, eyeing Roger de Courcey and seemingly wondering if his bear should sign too.

'One would have thought, the way these celebrities spray their shots around, you might have done better,' said a fat man, balanced precariously on a shooting-stick.

'A ball just whizzed past my cheek,' exclaimed an attractive lady with a badly bloodshot eye. 'I positively felt the wind of it!' No denying, one thought instinctively, that her good eye must have been only inches away from registering what the cricketing world knows painfully as 'a pair'.

'A ball hit my trouser-leg,' complained an elderly gentleman, but no one took any notice of him. He was just a rub of the green.

As Henry Cooper had promised, Ian Botham *did* hit a long ball, but it was counting 3 from the first tee when it swung away, all of 300 yards. His first ball had streaked off low like a torpedo, heading for the gardens and a young girl spectator, peeping from her garden gate. In the next few seconds, heads appeared and disappeared from the gardens, suspecting that a second Botham ball was going to knock them down, like the Punch and Judy show.

But with his second tee shot somewhere up near the first green, Ian ran over and recovered his first ball from the young girl and her friend, and agreed to have his photograph taken with each of them in turn at the garden gate. So much better than a mere autograph!

As I was leaving the clubhouse, I was surprised by a charming old lady rushing up to me with ball-point pen and programme. She thrust them into my whiskers and asked me to sign.

'What would you have me sign?' I asked her.

'Why, David Kossoff, of course!' she replied conspiratorially.

I feel sure I spelt it correctly. But hurriedly scribbled autographs are notoriously difficult to decipher, aren't they? And I know for a fact that Arnold Palmer once signed a paper napkin, disintegrating under his pen. Anyway, she got more than the others, didn't she?

12   Talking to the Ball

Do fishermen – fishing alone – talk to the fish they are trying to catch? In *The Old Man and the Sea* (Ernest Hemingway's story of a Cuban fisherman's struggle with a great marlin), the old man talked repeatedly to the giant fish. For two long days, as the marlin pulled the old man's skiff out to sea, he did so. Perhaps because there was no one else on hand to talk with and confide his hopes in, and perhaps because talking to a fish is better than talking to no one at all. Of course, the fact that fishermen often fish alone seems to offer an excuse for this sort of behaviour. But what of golfers habitually talking to golf balls?

Golfers seem to be much more addicted to this type of illogical one-way conversation than other sportsmen. But if you cavil at this statement, take a quick look with me at some other sports. Cricketers don't talk to a cricket ball or footballers to a football. True, rugby forwards may offer the odd, polite word or two as the ball is eased into the scrum; but most of the chat that takes place in the scrum is of a much more personal nature. Indeed, I once heard a lady spectator ask: 'Is that beehive thing a place where men put their heads together secretly to swap dirty jokes?'

That bowlers – both flat and crown green – talk to their bowls is evident enough as we watch and hear them at play. Employing a great deal of 'Body English', they chase excitedly down the green, commanding their running bowl to 'Get on!' – 'Ease up!' – 'Hurry!' – 'Whoa!' or similar orders. Bowlers come next to golfers, I think, in one-way chat of this illogical nature. But what of others? Do archers talk to their arrows? Caber-tossers to their cabers? Badminton players to their shuttlecocks? I doubt it.

As one grows older, one imagines that talking to golf balls on the links has become much more prevalent in the game than ever before. But maybe it's because golf – always a game for the emotions – becomes more emotional as the pressures increase. Eighteen holes of the rugged old stuff play havoc with our wrought-up feelings, and it would be a very cool fellow who refrained from yelling commands at his ball as it left the clubface. Watching the leading professionals on TV, we hear them demanding the ball to 'Cut!' or 'Get down!' or 'Sit!', as though, in the latter instance, they had entered a golf ball in dog-obedience trials. On the greens, they're everlastingly yelling 'Break!' or 'Go in!', as if the ball were equipped with ears and an understanding of golfing terms. Chip-shots and trap-shots are similarly shouted at to 'Get in!' And among the more optimistic pros, even long irons are given the same command, as though holing out from long distance were a mere modern-day formality.

Caddies, too, are prone to ball-talking. I recall Sam Snead writing of one, named O'Brien, who caddied for him in his play-off against Ben Hogan in the Masters in 1956.

'I hit a good putt and when I looked up, there's my caddie, O'Brien. He's standing over the ball, yellin', "Git in, git in," and waving at the ball with his hand. I was about to die 'cause I was sure that damned O'Brien would hit the ball with his hand.

'I left that green tied with Ben and said to O'Brien, "If you'd a-hit that ball with your hand, I'd have buried you right in that there green." '

One of Snead's favourite expressions when faced with a trying putt was 'Baby needs a new pair of shoes!' This was an expression common among American caddies which appealed to Sam's sense of humour. Using it enabled him to overcome any nervousness he might feel. The 'Baby' endearment is now pretty commonplace among golfers who talk to the ball. Lee Trevino uses it frequently, perhaps saying, as his ball heads for a sand-trap, 'Don't go in there, Baby! You'll get yourself all covered in sand.' Of course, Trevino talks non-stop to the ball and is famed throughout the golfing world for saying: 'You can talk to a fade, but a hook won't listen.' Many handicap golfers might add that they have talked to a fade until they became hoarse without getting the slightest response, the word 'fade' not being synonymous with 'control' for them.

Although talk between a golfer and his ball is almost exclusively one-way, there are times when the golf ball, too, seems determined to express an opinion. Such an occasion was that when Seve Ballesteros made his final putt in the 1984 Open at St Andrews. With thousands of voices urging it on, Seve's ball hung on the very lip of the hole and threatened to stay there. But as a tremendous roar and sigh rose from the crowd and hung in anticipation right round the green, it suddenly decided to become a champion among golf balls and do a little talking of its own. 'Hello!' it said. 'Here's a hole. Let's drop in!' And – like someone calling for afternoon tea – in it dropped, with Seve excitedly punching the air again and again in unconcealed boyish delight.

Sadly, sometimes golf balls take it upon themselves to answer back. Bobby Jones had such a ball in a match which he lost to Chick Evans. 'I'll never understand my own putt,' said Bobby, 'which hit the cup, ran clear around it, and came out on the same side as I was, and looked me in the eyes, and said: "You're licked!" '

13   Doing What Comes Naturally

Often when I'm sitting in the barber's chair, getting myself prettied up, the talk turns to golf. Chipping from a tangle of rough round my left ear, my barber removes a large divot and, at the same time, confesses to feeling absolutely out of it whenever he reads the finer points of scientific and technical golf. He says these are mysteries he cannot fathom.

'It's all very well for the experts to tell us that our swing plane will be no good if our knees are too flexed, or that our right hip should rotate during the backswing,' he declares, 'but what they don't seem to understand is that most of us wouldn't know a flexed knee or a rotating hip if we saw one. Can *you* spot a rotating hip when it's on the move?'

'Only in a belly dancer,' I said.

'What do you suppose would happen if I worried about flexing my knees or rotating my right hip as I snip around this rosebud ear of yours?'

No answer.

But as I sneak a look in the mirror, my ear seems suddenly at risk, and I hope his bantering tone won't destroy his concentration and lead to bits of ear on the floor or even complete amputation. I am as attached to that ear as it is to me. It's one of an antique pair I've worn for years. Besides, the thought of playing in the monthly medal bandaged like Van Gogh is rather disquieting.

'I hope you won't cut it off.'

'You needn't worry, sir. We haven't lost an ear for at least a fortnight. My scissors swing naturally without a thought of technique.'

Lovely indeed, as I remember them now, to see the natural swingers striking the ball by instinct, seemingly without a care in the world, as though they were out in the countryside with a dog, whacking fallen fir-cones with a stick.

Those who were lucky enough to see him in his tournament days will agree that Harry Bradshaw, the happy Irishman from Portmarnock, was a superb example of the natural golf swing. He was the quintessence of easy-going endeavour and doing what comes naturally. So much so, that whenever I accompanied him on the links, I was reminded of the lady who said: 'I never know which fairway I'm playing on. I simply bat the ball around till I finally wind up back at the clubhouse!' If Harry doesn't mind my saying so, there existed between them a similar tranquillity of mind, if not of purpose.

Of course, Harry was no stylist. In neither method of swing nor sartorial elegance did he tend to overdo things. Employing a somewhat agricultural action, in which three fingers of his right hand overlapped the left, he gave the ball a grand, carefree wallop, hard and invariably dead straight. And he thought of nothing more than that, I'm sure. Of his unorthodox grip, when asked why he adopted it, he replied: 'Be Gob, m'roight hand is so strong Oi could kill a feller with ut!'

Apart from playing as easily as falling off a tee-peg, the natural golfers had the gift of imparting their ideas in undecorated phrases. To the golfer who wanted to know how he could get more length into his shots, Ted Ray declared: 'Hit it a damned sight harder, mate!' And Tommy Armour was equally forthright with his: 'Whack the hell out of the ball with the right hand.' No need to consult diagrams or the medical dictionary to understand those instructions.

Scotland's George Duncan was another natural genius of swing and one of the fastest players ever to take up his stance and clip the ball away. Moreover, his down-to-earth advice on the correct stance was so simple to understand that no man (not even my barber) could fail to follow it by adopting the wrong position.

Ben Travers, novelist and playwright of *Cuckoo in the Nest* and *Rookery Nook* fame, told a humorous story to illustrate George's ideas. Tom Webster, the *Daily Mail* sports cartoonist, who was a friend of Travers, took him to play golf one Sunday afternoon at a suburban course. At lunch they were joined by a stranger whose name Travers failed to catch but whom Webster said was to play with them after lunch.

On the way to the first tee, Travers discovered that his unknown threesome opponent was none other than the great George Duncan!

'Oh, thanks very much,' said Travers. 'I'll watch.'

But Duncan wouldn't hear of that. He insisted on Travers taking part in the match. So he did as he was told and stepped onto the tee to drive off.

'No, no,' said Duncan. 'You're standing all wrong.'

In dour Scottish earnestness, he gave his directions.

'Stand to pee – and in your imagination let your urine fall six inches behind the ball, and you'll be in the correct stance for the drive.'

Travers obeyed orders and hit the ball about thirty yards along the ground.

Travers never did get the hang of it. But soon afterwards he asked Duncan whether he taught many ladies to play the game, and thus became a privileged spectator.

14 Playing the Oddities

'Little do we know wot lays afore us!' said Mrs Harris to Mrs Gamp. And Mrs Gamp, in her comical Dickens lingo, replied: 'Not much, it's true, but more than you suppoge.'

These *Martin Chuzzlewit* ladies weren't talking of golf, of course, but their remarks provide a teeing-off point to the psychological game, no matter where or by whom the round is played.

Little did Bernhard Langer know 'wot lay afore' him in the Benson & Hedges International Open at Fulford. As you know, by a capricious kind of fate, one of his short approaches finished up a tree, resting in a fork of the branches some ten feet above normal divot level and, as Mrs Gamp observed, it was more than he or anyone else 'suppoged' would happen. What's more, the spectacle of Langer shinning up the tree, finding a stance among the branches and then chipping out successfully to the green, was altogether more than on-the-spot spectators and TV viewers 'suppoged' was possible.

If there's a tendency to be cocksure about what sort of lie we might expect in golf, this Langer sermon from his leafy pulpit instantly dispels it. So many unexpected things can happen in a round of golf that it should come as no surprise to find ourselves barefoot, having removed a shoe and sock to play from a watery creek. Incidentally, this brave step was taken by a former British Amateur champion in the Masters at Augusta. Deciding his ball was playable in the water at the thirteenth, he removed his left shoe and sock and rolled his trouser above the knee. Then, placing his bare foot on the bank of the brook, he stuck his still-shod right foot into the water!

The eminent name of Arnold Palmer has long been synonymous in the golfing mind with recovery shots and heroics from bird's-nest territory. Urged on by his own personal 'army' (that stampeding, bolstering-up, whooping mass of gallerites who look to him affectionately for eagle and birdie charges), Arnie is always prepared to try to make something out of nothing. Give him the merest chink through the trees, and he'll gamble on recovery, and somehow miraculously achieve it. Some years ago his ball, like Langer's, got stuck up a gum-tree in Australia and, being Arnie, he climbed the tree and whacked it down with his usual flair and success. His golfing psychology eschews the routine routes of fairway driving to the point of monotony. After an almighty, uninhibited crack at the ball, he plays dynamics from beech, elm and fir, combined with charming variations from heather, gorse and bramble.

Similarly, Seve Ballesteros produces outrageous recovery shots just when he needs them most, and it would be no surprise to see him hop up a tree and, with characteristic unconcern, hammer his way out like the greater spotted woodpecker.

A young professional's odd experience in the Coral Classic Golf Tournament at Royal Porthcawl was enough to strike fear into the bravest golfing heart.

Playing in his first tournament of the season, Andrew Limb, 21, assistant professional at Lindrick, reached the ninth tee with the respectable score of 2 over par. But driving from the 9th (371 yards), he put his ball into deep rough on the right of the fairway – and then failed to find it. He walked back to the tee and played again, and put his ball into the same deep rough on the right – and again failed to find it. He did this twice more, his tee-shot always finishing in the deep rough on the right, and the ball always remaining lost. On his fifth drive (playing 9 from the tee), he found his ball and finally holed out in 12.

Normally, it takes between ten and fifteen minutes to play Royal Porthcawl's ninth hole, but it took Andrew Limb forty-five minutes, mostly accounted for by searching for the balls and, of course, walking back, walking back, walking back, walking back.

The ninth fairway and the general landscape thereabouts must have become as familiar to Andrew as those at Lindrick, or even the garden path or pattern on his bedroom carpet at home. The same old divot marks, the same infernal rough, the same old walk back, the same old tee and, to make matters worse, four brand new balls refusing to come out and show themselves, like fairies at the bottom of the garden.

Andrew lost another ball, the sixth altogether (he had lost a ball earlier in his round before losing four at the 9th), and he decided he wasn't going to walk back again. 'I just couldn't face another walk back to the tee,' he said.

So, like the Wodehouse cat that had a banana aimed at it as it was entering a room, Andrew decided to withdraw.

In a golfing career teeming with crackerjack shots, Bobby Jones once played a remarkable recovery shot that may never be duplicated.

He arrived at his ball to find it tucked inside an old shoe that had been thrown into a wheelbarrow. It was a ticklish problem to know what to do. Some observers thought it couldn't be played from where it lay; others thought it could. But at length Bobby decided to take a chance and play from the wheelbarrow.

He made a determined attack on the shoe with his niblick – just socked the shoe hard – and, observing both shoe and ball pitch on the green, saw his ball roll to within holeable distance. And I'm happy to tell you that, after that sensational shot, the incomparable Bobby smoothly slid his putt down for a 4!

15 Switching the Greens

During the night a boisterous wind swept across the autumnal links and demonstrated to golfers (tucked up in bed and snoring outrageously) how to pitch onto the eighteenth green. Leaf upon leaf was torn unceremoniously from the trees and pitched at the flagstick, so that by morning light the whole of the putting surface was covered with a brownish-yellow carpet, like seaweed left behind on the seashore. Thousands of leaves that no golfer, no matter how adroit with his putter, could have hoped to negotiate in fewer than half a dozen strokes. Indeed, had he been required to play on the green before the greenkeeper arrived, he would have counted himself fortunate just to *find* his ball, let alone hole it.

Early-morning golfers pay scant attention to the green-keeper's switching of the greens, yet he's the fellow who makes play possible by returning the putting surfaces to respectability, from fallen leaves and wormcast encumbrance. He swings his magic wand that backward and forward switches its long tail, known in the greenkeeper's book as a 'telescopic switch'. It looks like a fishing-rod and, seeing him carrying it over his shoulder as he moves from green to green, one might suspect him of playing truant and sneaking off from the golf links in favour of the running stream. Its lightweight qualities are something that would please a fly-fisherman and add to the pleasure of hooking and playing a trout or salmon. But, though of fishing-rod appearance, it's simply a light handle about seven feet long with a fibreglass, pencil-slim rod sliding easily inside. The rod is of similar length to the handle and makes a switch of about fourteen feet in all, easily adjustable to the required length.

Watching the greenkeeper clearing up leaves with his switch makes one think how easy it is. Would that we golfers could match the easy repetitive movement of his swing! Swish, swish, it goes, with a sound like quiet waves pushing at fine shingle.

'It is utterly impossible for any golfer to play good golf without a swing that will repeat,' says Ben Hogan in *The Modern Fundamentals of Golf*. Well, here's a good example. The greenkeeper's actions not only repeat effortlessly, but he obviously gives no thought to the precise gripping of the switch: neither overlapping nor interlocking, nor making a conscious distinction of backward and forward swings. Yet every leaf is driven obediently and unfailingly into line. What would we golfers give for a simple repeating swing like that? We who, as Sir Walter Simpson said, teach ourselves crippled swings by driving at daisies and make ourselves knock-kneed so that we stand like a crab when addressing the ball. If only we could swing a club as the greenkeeper swings his switch! See him dominate a single leaf! And this, mark you, with a fourteen-foot shaft! What fine confidence! What admirable technique and control!

The other day, in contemplative mood on my exercise bike, I thought of Sandy Lyle being interviewed by Clive Clark on TV, and of an interesting remark of Sandy's.

'You're very long off the tee, Sandy,' said Clive. 'Where does all the length come from?'

'I think it comes from doing a lot of work on the course when I was young,' replied Sandy. 'I spent a lot of time switching the greens. The length comes from powerful shoulders and a full shoulder turn. Switching the greens developed good muscles and, even more helpful, a very full shoulder turn.'

Now this was a profound observation by Sandy, for one of Ben Hogan's fundamentals in his book is the need for the golfer to make a *full* shoulder turn. The more he or she turns the shoulders, the better.

'Most golfers think they make a full shoulder turn going back, and they would challenge you if you claimed they didn't, but the truth is that few golfers really complete their shoulder turn,' says Ben. In his opinion, golfers stop when they're about half-way round, and then, in order to get further back, break the left arm. A good way to check if you're making a full turn, says Ben, is to see if your chin hits against your left shoulder. Hogan's golf shirts proved the point about his chin by showing a worn spot at that precise area.

However, I think we can take it for granted that the

greenkeeper studies no books of instructions written by Telescope Switch champions in collaboration with their ghosts. He doesn't worry about two Vs pointing at his shoulder; doesn't bother to keep his chin behind the leaves, bring his left knee in past them or keep strictly to an inside-out path as he whacks a wormcast. His thoughts are elsewhere. Maybe with an anticipated cup of coffee and a large jam doughnut. Who knows?

Perhaps – if he's a poetic greenkeeper – on those greens away from trees and leaves, he's given to studying the footprints and ball-tracks left behind in the silvery dew by early morning 'dewsweeper' golfers. Doubtless at a glance he can see where an approach-putt fell woefully short and the next slid too far past the hole. Three putts recorded in the tell-tale dew. What's more, a technical Sherlock Holmes would point to those footprints to prove that the putting-stance was grotesquely pigeon-toed and far from academic. Indeed, just between ourselves, those early birdie 'dewsweeper' golfers who play before the greenkeeper arrives have reason to be grateful that he flicks a telescopic switch – and not an instamatic camera ...

16   Advantages of Greenside Ponds

Once upon a time, a pond alongside a short hole was de-weeded and de-balled and, in the cleaning-out process, an old pitching club and three putters were recovered. One of the putters was thought to be worthy of a replacement shaft and later repaid its benefactor by holing out from all over the place, distance being no object, as the young lad said who did his courting on roller-skates. Of course, no one knew just how long the putter had rested in its muddy grave at the bottom of the pond or who had put it there, or why, and one could only assume that its former owner had been some red-eared fellow given to hysterical outbursts over the missing of short putts.

Of all clubs in the bag, the poor old putter is the one most often thrown in anger, and nothing is easier to the disenchanted golfer than to hurl it into a pond. Which is what Australian David Graham might have done in the 1981 Lancôme Trophy, for there was a pond ready and waiting beside the last green at St-Nom la Breteche, and the temptation to dump his putter into it must have been hard to resist. After all, he'd missed five putts of six feet or under and, on his own admission, would have scored in the mid 60s if he'd putted at all decently. But, instead, he displayed a fine forbearance and self-control in *giving away* his putter to a young spectator.

A young 12-handicap Frenchman from Dijon was the lucky though somewhat unworthy recipient, for by all accounts he was a club-destroyer who confessed that, the previous week-end, after a bad day on the greens, he'd snapped his own putter across his knee.

Such brutal treatment of clubs is rare in the game today, for golfers don't batter their clubs or throw them around as they used to. Tempers aren't as hot as they were in the old days, or perhaps clubs are a bit too expensive now to manhandle or heave into the nearest pond. Young Frenchmen excepted, golf isn't the explosive and dramatic game it used to be.

Take, for example, the match in which Bobby Jones met Eben Byers, one-time American champion of the amateur game. This is what Bobby said about it.

'Mr Byers and I played terribly. He was a veteran and I was a youngster, but we expressed our feelings in exactly the same way – when we missed a shot we threw the club away. I think the main reason I beat him was because he ran out of clubs first. Somebody behind us said later that we looked like a juggling act.'

So you see. Time was when, even in championship play, club-throwing was a regular form of exercise, practised by old and young alike. If you missed a pitch, you slung your niblick into the nearest ditch. If you muffed a putt, without a thought of where the next putter was coming from, you upped and cracked the shaft across your knee. When you went out for a round, it wasn't so much a question of how many strokes you were going to take as how many clubs you were likely to lose.

In his younger days, Henry Longhurst thought the act of throwing a club was 'the most exquisitely satisfying in the world of golf', and he declared that the unique whirring sound, 'reminiscent of a passing flock of starlings', was without parallel in sport.

Yet another golf writer, H.N. Wethered, gave us one of the best club-throwing stories from the old days. For anyone who feels a tendency to be bored with what is predictable in golf, it's a classic of its kind, eminently satisfying, though admittedly rather Machiavellian.

An actor was trying to drive across a pool in front of the first tee but had put his first and second shots into the water. Less temperamental golfers would doubtless have teed another ball, but the actor cried: 'Give me all the balls, caddie!' – and flung them into the water. 'Take these balls, O Pond!' he declaimed loudly. Then the clubs followed: 'And these clubs, O Pond!' Unfortunately at this crisis the caddie laughed and was thrown in as well. 'And this caddie, too, O Pond!'

The temptation of greenside ponds is a cross we golfers have to bear. Cricketers don't fling their bats into the crowd or give them away to spectators. Lawn tennis players are equally frugal and conservative, and footballers likewise. I've no wish to balance things in their favour, but I can't help wondering if they'd succumb to the temptations if ponds were available. Would McEnroe and Nastase make an indecent splash with balls or racquets if there was a pond alongside the centre court? And, following an uncharacteristic duck, would Botham be tempted with his big heavyweight bat at the Oval or Lord's ponds?

All very speculative of course, but before I take my leave of you to count my tee-pegs, there's one final pond I must mention. It was spoken of before the district attorney in the grand jury room, and I quote it to show that ponds on American courses are just as advantageous as our own.

The accused was explaining how his opponent on the course kept crying out to him as he addressed his ball: 'Keep your head down, keep your head down!' Driven to desperation by this continual babel of unwanted advice, the accused told how, at the fifteenth hole, while his opponent was standing on the edge of a pool looking for a ball, he gave him a pat on the back – and he fell in. He said he believed his opponent had decided to commit suicide for the good of mankind and, quite naturally, he felt obliged to assist him in his purpose by holding his head under the water.

'And what did you say while you were assisting him?' asked the district attorney.

'Keep your head down, keep your head down!' replied the accused.

17 *One of the Early Birds*

Some things are hard to recall, but playing golf in the early morning isn't. Once you've experienced it, it's the sort of thing you couldn't forget in a million years. For a start, there's the excitement of going to bed at night knowing that first thing in the morning you'll be hitting a golf ball. 'You must wake and call me early, call me early, mother dear,' said Tennyson, and though he was writing of the May Queen, he could just as easily have been anticipating early morning golf.

In my teens, I used to wake from dreams of eighteen consecutive holes in one and, getting out of bed at 4.30, walk three miles over country roads without meeting a single soul. And all the way to the links there was something of interest to watch. Rabbits bobbing their wee white tails in and out of hedges, horses polishing their noses on five-barred gates, and cows casting quizzical, reproving glances at me for daring to be abroad so early in the morning. The lovely freshness and stillness of the morning air, the wonder of the sky at sunrise, the clear sound of birdsong and the dawn chorus. And then, when I reached the links, the sheer joy and excitement of having the whole place to myself.

I liked to make a point of getting on the first tee before six o'clock. That used to give me about an hour and a half for my round, or however many holes I could manage to play. Sometimes I used to hit two balls from each tee, scoring one against the other, and I always found it an admirable method of practice. Though you may not know it, it's an idea endorsed by famous golfers. Harry Vardon employed it in the early days of golf, when opponents weren't easy to come by. He said he got lots of fun out of it. For instance, if he got two or three holes up on himself, the losing half of him would resolutely attack the winning half in an effort to square the match. Indeed, Harry writes of a fanatical golfer who was so impressed with this method of play that he always insisted on using two bags of clubs. One set was old, the other quite new, and he pitted them against one another without a thought of cheating or the trouble involved. What's more – get this – he carried both bags himself! A veritable Jekyll and Hyde of the links, to whom change of club if not of countenance came quite readily.

Max Faulkner was another famous player who used the two-ball method whilst playing alone, and praised its qualities. The great Ben Hogan made a habit of playing by himself and prepared for his Open win in 1953 at Carnoustie in this way. Maybe he played one ball against another, too. John Ball, the famous amateur, played alone at Hoylake, often playing the course backwards. Possibly he was another who used two balls, and found that his second ball was sterner opposition than that of an opponent. Playing by yourself gives you the opportunity to be free of distractions and so allow you to size up a course's problems more thoroughly.

I must get back to the main theme of early-morning golf, but first let me advise you to try out the two-ball idea for, if taken seriously, it's a splendid form of training. But – please – one set of clubs only, not two – or you'll be in sight of your last knockings inside six months …

At different periods of my golfing life, I've continued to rise early and rush away to the waiting, deserted links. There's a serenity and solitude soon after sunrise, and it's the most peaceful place to be out there alone from tee to green. The greenkeepers are still in bed, the heavy dew and wormcasts uncleared by their swish-sticks, and putting and judging the pace of the greens are at their most unpredictable moment. But what a subject here for an artistic photographer! Each stance recorded in detail in the dew's tell-tale tracks. Each putt indicating success (or the lack of it) as the silvery trails lead into or past the hole. What, I wonder, does the first man to follow in our footsteps think of the patterns? Is he discerning enough to assess our score? Does he smile at all the zigzag trolley-wheel tracks from tee to rough, back to fairway, and then to rough again? Perhaps, on second thoughts, photographs should not be taken, however artistic they might be. The early morning golfer's secrets would be too sharply exposed. The outcome would be like a game of chess in which every move is recorded and condemned in retrospect.

But mark this, you golfers who like to roll over and pull the duvet to your ears. Early morning golf is a great thing for the appetite. Nine holes before breakfast make a fellow roar like feeding time at the Zoo when they slip the old bacon and eggs under his whiskers.

As I've got older, I've got lazy. Instead of walking to the links and sniffing the early morning air, I've gone by car, and you miss a lot when you do things the easy way and too quickly. But whether you walk or sit in a car or astride a camel, the nip of the air and the joy of hitting a golf ball will be waiting for you when you arrive. And perhaps the greatest thrill of all will come when you walk off the eighteenth green and bump into someone who, at 8.30, is just arriving at the course, priding himself on being the early birdie.

Just watch his mouth sag open as you say that you drove off before six and are now off home to breakfast. It's the sort of thing that's guaranteed to drive the poor old sluggards crazy ...

18 In Praise of Young Caddies

Young boys rarely caddie these days, and more's the pity. They used to keep golfers company for an hour or two, make friends and memories, and then – especially on unfamiliar courses – suddenly vanish away and never be met with again.

These young boys, some not much bigger than the golf bag, knew a lot about the game and carried with professional competence. They were magicians at spying out the right line on the greens, so that the hole opened up unexpectedly, like a stage trapdoor, to let the ball drop in, and, as H.G. Hutchinson said, 'always able to put into your hand the right club, almost without your asking for it'.

On the other hand, some of the little beggars were practically useless. Dreaming of mountains of eggs and bacon, because they'd rushed to the links without breakfast. Continually fiddling with potato crisps or messing about with crackly toffee-papers as we poised ourselves over a vital putt. Or worse still, catching fieldmice or big fat toads and slipping them secretly into the golf-bag pocket, to take away with them when the round was over – and then forgetting!

All this might sound pretty melodramatic, but it was a great relief to see some of the more unconventional ones buzz off, like troublesome hornets, never to sting us again – we hoped. But, on the whole, the young caddies were dedicated to club-carrying, did a grand job of work and were more charming than tiresome in the process.

Apart from one's own personal reminiscences, I like to think of those *nine* young caddies who shared Henry Longhurst's bag at Hong Kong and insisted on accompanying him *en masse* for a few cents apiece. Henry thought it was like taking a kindergarten for a walk – and the lies he got were outstanding.

'The only reason I didn't find it actually on a tee-peg in the rough was that the boys possessed no tee-pegs.'

Longhurst met up with 'a quite enchanting little villain' at the Masjid-i-Sulaiman Golf Club in the foothills of Persia. So did I, a year or so before Longhurst. Maybe his young villain was the same enchanting villain who carried for me, for our experiences were very much alike.

My tiny, ever-smiling Persian boy made tees from mud, for the bare, rocklike ground was impossible to push a tee-peg into. From a roll of plasticine-like mud always kept at the ready, he fashioned a kind of whipped-cream walnut and set my ball upon it. When I lost a ball in that mountainous terrain (where a drive goes 400 yards because of the almost never-ending run on the ball), it might be lost in the very place I couldn't look. That's to say, concealed inside the boy's large wad of mud-plasticine, somewhere within the folds of his ankle-length nightshirt!

But my young Persian caddie flashed his smiles with sudden splendour, stringing them across the fairways like precious pearls. Hassan's sweetmeats could not have been sweeter and, never sparing himself, he prayed for my putts to drop. A young-old dog for a hard Persian road, he told me to use my putter to recover from a bone-dry, shallow-lipped bunker, and it worked like a dream. Many years later, I found Henry Cotton offering the same tip!

Like Longhurst in Hong Kong, I never had a bad lie the whole day through. I fancy my lad was equally adroit with his barefoot toes as with his whipped-cream-walnut fingers. At all events, I loved his performance and became enchanted, for he was more friend and confidant than native-boy caddie. Shortly after saying goodbye, I was ticked off by a club member for overpayment. He feared my generosity could lead to inflated caddie-fees. At Persian currency exchange rates, it seemed I'd given the lad about sixpence instead of the customary threepence.

Miss Joyce Wethered had her clubs carried at Sunningdale many years ago by a boy who knew nothing of the game. Little more than ten years' old, he'd been told by other boys that there were rich pickings to be had on the golf course. It was ironic, I think, for him to make his début paired with Miss Wethered, a raw beginner with one so finely trained. He neither knew where to stand nor recognized one club from another. When Miss

Wethered requested her mashie-niblick, he thrust the bag under her nose and left her to choose. What else could he do?

At the end of the day, Miss Wethered said, though not unkindly, 'You're the worst caddie I've ever had!' But he was not upset, for the highlights of his day bore little relation to the finer points of golf. His joy came from the bread and cheese and pickles at lunchtime, and from the two shining half-crowns Miss Wethered gave him for his morning and afternoon stint. No one could have been happier, but he took care not to caddie again.

You may wonder how I know all this. Well, Frank Readings, the raw young caddie, took up golf on retirement, is now turned seventy and, more power to his elbow, thumps the ball like Jack Dempsey. Moreover, his future intentions can be summed up in Dempsey's own words: 'Keep punching.'

Up to his retirement, Frank always thought golf a silly game, played by cissies, but he's now among its most dedicated supporters and, of course, he has a claim to fame most of us would enjoy. He carried the clubs of the greatest woman golfer the game has known. Very few can say as much.

By a lucky chance, in the streets of Gullane, Bernard Darwin once picked up 'a great little boy'. When their partnership and the Oxford and Cambridge Golf Society tour ended, Darwin said he would rather have pasted in his book of memories a photograph of 'the brown, grinning, resolute little face of my caddie' than that of any group of players. Darwin's young boy was keen on golf, but keener still on birds and beasts, 'so that a round with him resembled, to borrow a famous title, a naturalist's voyage round the world'. For instance, he dragged Darwin far into the rough at Gullane to show him a plover's nest with eggs in it. And on another detour, it was a lark's nest. But the boy was happiest of all at Archerfield (the leaning, windswept woods of Muirfield).

'When he first came through the curtain of woods into that entrancing spot, he was, for the space of almost two holes, dumb with ecstasy. Then he broke out: "This is a bonny wee place. You can see nothing of the rabbits but their wee white tails." '

Dashing away from Darwin for a moment, he reappeared holding a baby plover in each of his pudgy brown hands. 'I should add,' wrote Darwin, in his nostalgic, incomparable piece in *The Times*, 'that he replaced them, very tenderly, whence they came.'

No simple naturalist, but a boy of action, too. When Darwin's companion hooked a ball into a neighbouring garden, 'of which the owner was declared to be a fire-eater who allowed no balls to be retrieved', he crept, bending low, under the stone wall, over barbed wire, casting wary glances at the house, and reappeared in triumph with the ball, sucking a wounded finger.

'Some day I shall be able to boast that a great man once carried my clubs,' said Darwin.

Alas, the joys of the boy caddies are no more. They've been replaced by the ubiquitous, impersonal golf-trolley. And – I ask you – how can a trolley drag you off into the rough to peep at eggs in a plover's nest or retrieve a ball from a fire-eater's garden?

19   Make it Tough

However good a golfer may be, there comes a time when he pokes one off the line and ends up in the jungle. Everybody does it. Jack Nicklaus, Arnold Palmer, Tom Watson, Seve Ballesteros, Willie Wigglesworth – all at one time or another finish up in the gorse bushes, wondering how in the name of Mrs O'Leary's cow they're going to get out. But they do get out. Often with superb recovery shots that leave us gasping with astonishment. And in the excitement of the moment we seldom give a single thought to the hours of practice that may have preceded the shot. For that's a side of the game we rarely see. Crack golfers practising the art of recovering from bad lies, with all the perserverance of Alice trying to find her way out of Wonderland ...

Well, as it happened, I'd lifted little Gene Sarazen down from the shelf and, having blown the dust from him, I noticed that he said: 'The cardinal error which players commit today when they practise is to nudge each shot on to a perfect lie. You must practise hitting balls out of fair, poor and downright bad lies.'

So what did I do? I upped and went like a curate with a nannygoat behind him, shinned up a lofty tree overlooking the seventeenth green and, selecting a stance between the branches, began practising recovery shots for all I was worth.

Seriously though, there's a lot in what Gene says. Far too many players make a habit of practising dead-easy lies from the fairway, instead of tough ones from the rough. What's more, they make the mistake of using the clubs with which they're most proficient, rather than those they find hardest to handle. After all, what's the good of hitting a stream of shots with a 3-wood or 3-iron, each one from a well-perched-up lie, when you could use those clubs to a nicety before you started? And what's the sense in bashing a lot of sand out of the easiest bunker on the course? Why not let your hair down and vary your routine with half a dozen stinkers from the bottom of a ditch? And – after wiping the mud out of your eye, like the hero you are – why not try another half-dozen from a crippling position under the spreading chestnut tree?

History has it that Francis Ouimet used to relieve the monotony of practice sessions by hitting iron shots to the green from behind a large tree. In this way, he had to not only judge the distance to the stick – which is the usual thing – but also the height of the tree. Scotland's own Jimmy Braid had no equal at recovering from bad places. Given a niblick, he could recover from anywhere, as Walton Heath's scars will testify to this day. And, of course, one can say the same of Walter Hagen. Indeed, it's been said often that Hagen put himself into trouble deliberately, just for the thrill of showing the customers what he could do with recoveries.

Tom Watson and Seve Ballesteros are modern-day counterparts of the older champions. Watson's shot that won him the 1982 US Open at Pebble Beach, when he chipped into the hole for a miracle birdie from rough behind the seventeenth green, has been much publicized, but the most unremarked feature of it was the hours he'd spent practisting and perfecting delicate little pitches from the rough. Seve Ballesteros makes marvellous recoveries from jungle country, but not, I'm sure, without having practised recovery possibilities from the worst places, car-parks included!

Come then. Let's have a look at one or two trying situations and decide what should be done with them. For example, here, in a perfectly obnoxious place deep in a clump of heather, is where your tee shot has come to rest. How are you to get it out? Well, the obvious answer is, the next time you practise, practise in the heather and find out! And keep on banging them out of the filthy stuff until you feel confident that, should you poke one there again (as you doubtless will), you'll have a pretty good chance of getting out at the first attempt.

To give another example, here, at the base of an old oak, is where your ball has come to rest. True, the ball lies well enough. But there's nowhere to stand. Well – find somewhere to stand! Arnold Palmer found somewhere to stand after he had hooked that shot into the fork of a gum-tree in Australia. Climbing twenty feet up the tree, he reversed the head of his l-iron and hammered the ball to the ground, chipped to the green and holed the putt. So why not place one foot between the roots, like that? And the other partly up the tree, like that? Very well, then, as Old Tom Morris used to say: 'Play wi' yer heid as well's yer hands.' Remember that it's easier to play a good recovery *after* the ball is back in play than from where you're standing – on one leg.

And, just between you and me, take care you don't tear the seat of your pants on that spiky little branch immediately behind you. For I know a chap who stood there before you, who speaks with considerable feeling on that very point ...

20 Desert Swings

Most golfers, be they professional, scratch or 'just scratching', are endeared to their putters and cherish them as much as Bobby Jones did his famous 'Calamity Jane' or Bobby Locke his hickory-shafted putting-stick that performed like a magic wand. My case is no exceptional one, for the putter to which I am endeared came into my possession when I was in the Iraqi Desert during the Second World War.

There, amongst a pile of miscellaneous rubbish and sports equipment lying idle in a tent, I was greatly surprised to see an aged canvas golf-bag. Now this, to an ardent golfer who for months had been unable to do anything more tangible than think of the game, was incredibly stimulating. Lifting the bag from its dim corner and shaking it warily in case of deadly scorpions, I tentatively pulled the zipper of the bag, and there beheld six steel-shafted clubs – brassie, spoon, 3-, 5-, and 7-irons, and the putter of which I have already spoken. I felt that the discovery, at not more than a few miles from Ur, was personally more electrifying than any of Sir Leonard Woolley's profound disclosures.

I made enquiries about the clubs and found no one interested in golf. The clubs had been left there ready to be discarded. I was very happy to think that 'in the nick of time', so to speak, I had come along to preserve this treasure from a most unworthy end. To imagine the wandering Arabs beating their camels or stirring iguana soup with a hickory spoon was to do the clubs and the Royal and Ancient Pastime a great disservice. During that afternoon, under the fierce Iraqi sun, I spent a delightful hour, swinging, admiring, exulting and making the desert sand fly from each iron in turn. Swinging the clubs was the most I could do, for there was no ball available either in or out of the bag.

For the next two years I zealously carried those clubs throughout my extensive travels. They went with me through

Iraq, Palestine, Syria and the Western Desert, and on to Sicily and Italy. If I couldn't get golf balls (as indeed I couldn't), at least I could swing. And, whenever the opportunity presented itself, swing I did. Though it may be thought an idle statement, and certainly no worthy achievement, I believe myself to be the only golfer who cut a divot at Bug-Bug whilst Rommel was being chased to Tunis by Monty and his Eighth Army. This is not to say that the Desert War was won with a brassie or spoon, of course, merely that, if Rommel had suddenly turned on his heel, I was waiting for him at the top of the swing with a firm interlocking grip.

During the long-drawn-out Italian campaign, I set about making a golf ball. I made it from barage-balloon elastic rope and, by pulling the ends of the elastic thread painstakingly around the core, managed to accomplish a creditable roundness. The next problem was to overcome the violent bounce of the ball, which, after much experiment, was checked by a cover of adhesive tape.

By this time, another golfer had come along, and together we constructed a couple of holes at each end of a restricted fairway about 150 yards long. In our off-duty moments, we tramped up and down this fairway (if you could call it *fair*!), engaged in foursome matches against the make-believe, august and inspiring company of Cotton and Locke. Mostly we used to average 4s – and I well remember that the course record stood at 68. Later we had the good fortune to meet an American airman who gave us a golf ball, and whose generosity undoubtedly helped to set a new record for the course. Early in the life of this American ball, we cut a few strokes off the old record – we lowered it to 65, I think – but we played with it so often that it became woefully egg-shaped, gaping and soft. We repaired it many times. We used to put it in a vice and squeeze it back to shape, patch up its cuts, and so on. If anyone had threatened its existence, we would have put aside golf clubs – and fixed bayonets …

21 *Second Nature*

One of the most irreverent sights in golf is the mutilation of smooth green fairways by the golf beginner's short irons. I recall one such assassin. A bookish, bespectacled sort of chap, more fitted to leaping about in meadows with a butterfly-net than tackling the game of golf, he seemed to enjoy nothing better than cutting up divots the size of muffins. So much so, someone gave him the nickname of 'Muffins' – and members would say, 'I see Muffins has been round this way again,' as they came upon half a dozen abandoned, muffin-sized divots on the fairway. For, though he obviously enjoyed heaving away at the ball and cutting up turf, he never bothered to replace it. Indeed, it got so bad with his continual criss-crossing of the fairways that a committeeman had to take him on one side and whack him on the shins with a sand iron. Things were better after that. You could still see where he'd been by the deep laceration in the turf, but no reasonably astute observer needed to be told that 'Muffins' ' muffins were back in place.

However, the point I want to stress about this spike-shod menace is that, no matter what disheartening experience befell him, he refused to yield. It took him a heck of a time to reach a stage of proficiency whereby he could knock the ball farther than the divot, but he stuck to it like fluff to a humbug. Nothing seemed to put him off, nothing discourage him. Fresh-air shots, sockets, very nearly cutting the ground from under his own two feet – they all came alike to him. He had an astonishing self-confidence and positively thrived on error and wearisome repetition.

'You cannot play scratch golf or better till you are as full of confidence as an egg is full of meat,' said Andrew Kirkaldy, old-time Scottish golfer and one of the most quoted the game has known. 'Andra' sometimes used an expression which is well worth repeating today. It was 'ball fright' – the player shouldn't allow himself to become frightened of the ball, he declared. 'A bit of contempt for the ball is a very good thing,' he said, and it's interesting to note that his cure for ball-fright was simply the act of swinging without a ball. 'If ever you go off your game,' he observed to one of his pupils, 'take an hour or two at swinging without even thinking about the ball.' However, I trust you'll notice that he said an *hour* or two – not a *swing* or two.

Andra was right. As soon as they find themselves face to face with a golf ball on a peg, some players are reduced to the consistency of unset jelly. Their confidence vanishes like smoke on the wind. The sight of the fearsome little white ball makes them want to bury their heads in the tee-box. Yet, rooted to the spot, they're incapable of doing anything more positive than crawling about on their hands and knees. Ball-fright has them in its clutches …

In order to regain some measure of poise, let us consider the simple trick of eating. Most of us do it three or four times a day and think nothing of it. And, I ask you, is golf any more difficult than eating? The average mouth, dropped open to the eating position, is a good deal smaller than the circumference of a golf ball. Yet, if we stopped to think about the action of eating, might we not miss our mouths altogether? Might we not spear the fork right through the cheek – and end up with mouth-fright? At any rate, I have yet to meet anyone who worried about the action of eating (as we worry about the action of golf), elbow into the body, correct wrist-break, shut-faced fork and so on.

The truth of the matter is that eating is second nature to us. We are supremely confident. It's merely a question of knowing where your mouth is – and finding it. Knowing, so to speak, that it's approximately an inch under the nose and midway between the ears.

So the next time we feel a loss of confidence, perhaps we should think of a hungry man attacking a juicy steak or spooning a custard pie, and then go ahead and tackle the golf ball with the same fine frenzy.

22 *Sinking Feeling*

Ben Hogan said that golf is one game and putting another. In his opinion, one game is played in the air and the other on the ground. Moreover, Ben blamed his inability to sink vital putts on what he called 'trouble between the ears'. By this I think he meant that he was suffering from a lack of confidence coupled with a slight attack of the heeby-jeebies. And, of course, when it comes to *not* getting the ball in the hole, the mighty Hogan isn't the only guy who couldn't achieve it, for most of us have been climbing up the flagsticks for longer than we care to remember.

Contrary to popular belief, the most confident of putters isn't to be found among the top professionals of the day. Instead, he's way down at the bottom of the golfing ladder, somewhere among the long-handicap brigade and that Happy Band of Warriors, the Bold Beginners. Perhaps a surprising pronouncement. Yet not without some substance when we consider what P.G. Wodehouse said on the same subject: 'A man who could retain through his golfing career the almost scornful confidence of the non-player would be unbeatable.' On that issue, only a brave man would cross niblicks with P.G.W.

Consider the case of the non-player, the uninitiated greenhorn, taking his first whack at a golf ball on the putting greens of Brighton or Blackpool. One would expect him to be the biggest duffer in creation, unable to tell the difference between one end of the putting stick and the other. Yet this is hardly so ...

Having been rather reluctantly drawn in to the game to make the number up, and told that the idea of the game is nothing more than knocking the ball into a hole some thirty or forty yards away, he says: 'Oh, so that's the set-up, is it? I always thought it was like billiards. Two for a cannon and three for a pot!'

Then, ignoring all the smooth bits of turf on the tee – and

carefully placing his ball in a nasty-looking divot mark, he astonishes everybody by knocking one a foot from the cup. Dead, so to speak, as a corpse, and equally as holeable.

So he's away with a 2, which would satisfy even the most seasoned golfer, yet he's not at all happy about it. The game seemed so simple and straightforward, he fully expected to hole out at the first stroke.

However, among non-players, this chap's performance, though admittedly pretty hot, is by no means unique.

Stand for a moment or two the next time you pass the putting greens at the seaside, and watch the old ladies having a go. They're positively deadly. You'll see old girls of seventy and eighty rolling putts stiff as whiskers from almost any distance. Indeed, these old girls have such an unbounded confidence in themselves, they invent a sort of single-handed style, with a putter in one hand and a handbag in the other.

Now one has to face facts, and what it amounts to is this. Compared with the raw beginner, the professional golfer is a hesitant bungler. It's true that he suffers the disadvantage of playing for money – often quite a stack of the filthy stuff on the roll of a single putt – but, even so, the sight of the poor fellow dithering over a short one is sheer agony. Scratching around like an old hen, he looks at the ball as though it were the first he'd ever seen, gazes at the hole as if he were expecting it to get up and walk away, and squints suspiciously along the line of putt. And the worst of it is that, after he's gone right through the whole rigmarole once, he's so infernally fastidious and nervous, he gets his caddie to go through it all again.

One can't help thinking that a golfer who could model his putting style on that of the old ladies would not only save himself a lot of trouble but strokes and heartaches, too. The old girls don't go down on their knees to squint along the line. Indeed, it's doubtful whether they could. It would be just too painful. No. They walk up to the ball, smack it into the tin and then resume their discourse …

Because, naturally enough, like old ladies the world over, as they play, they carry on the spiciest of conversations – ranging from what the Vicar said about the parrot to what the parrot somewhat surprisingly said about the Vicar!

23   Punching the Air

It will not have escaped your eagle eye, I'm sure, that in professional golf, where tensions rise high as a kite, 'bunches of fives' are increasingly popular as a means of expressing players' exuberance when vital putts drop agreeably out of sight. Of course, in referring to 'bunches of fives', I'm not thinking of one untidy 5 after another on the scorecard, but bunches of five fingers rolled up pugnaciously into clenched fists.

I can offer no better illustration of a famous 'bunch of fives' used to knockout effect in golf than that of Seve Ballesteros winning the Open at St Andrews and punching the air repeatedly as his birdie putt fell dramatically into the seventy-second hole. You will recall those superb Seve jabs, delivered with lightning, piston-like motion, followed immediately by several others that whizzed perilously close to his right ear, culminating in a final 'bunch of fives' raised on high, like the Statue of Liberty's torch at New York harbour entrance.

But even those excited Seve-gestures were subsequently overshadowed by an energetic display of shadow-boxing with both fists as Ballesteros sank an unbelievable putt to defeat Bernhard Langer on the final green in the Irish Open. Seve pummelled the air vigorously with one fast punch after another (a couple of which may have been low and beneath the belt!) as he gave vent to his unconcealable joy.

Does any bright lad know where all this punching of the air first began? Did golfers copy the by-play of footballers? For more than two decades, international footballers have celebrated the scoring of a goal by punching the air and leaping around like demented butterfly-catchers with angry wasps inside their knickers. They race wildly to the touchlines, fall to their knees and punch the air with frenzied abandon, as though the wasps had invaded no-go areas.

If footballers started this air-punching by-play, from whom

did *they* become addicted. From shadow-boxers? From tempestuous wives or jilted girl-friends? From ticktack bookies signalling the odds? From politicians at the hustings? From Mrs O'Leary demanding overdue rent? From enraged, purple-faced fat fellows running after buses that refuse to stop? 'Stop! Damn you! Stop!' But the bus-conductor, pretending he hasn't seen Purple-Face Fatty threatening him with a nasty 'bunch of fives', smiles to himself and runs his fingers through his loose change.

No matter whose fist it is, it shoots out and upward in joyful celebration. In athletics, making a fist of it is as commonplace as taking off one's tracksuit. Steve Cram's fist. Steve Ovett's fist. Seb Coe's fist. Fatima Whitbread hurls the javelin and then hurls up double fists of celebration. Jim Howard, high-jumper from the States, also flings up double fists, shooting them up alarmingly as though his armpits had suddenly caught fire.

Golf fists are everywhere to be seen, but space prevents my giving more than a few. A smiling Tom Kite at the Open at Sandwich acknowledged a telling birdie putt with a charming table-tennis-chop action with his fist. Very gentle. Almost no making-a-fist-of-it. Christy O'Connor, junior, made a rat-a-tat-tat fist as he sank a wicked putt for a desperate par. His raised fist went *one, two, three*, as if knocking urgently on the door of an Irish pub. Howard Clark went *punch, punch, punch*, as he floored his American opponent in the Ryder Cup. Sam Torrance, holing from eighteen feet to win the vital point in the Ryder Cup, put on the style by raising both fists aloft in an emotional celebration. Perhaps more than any other golfer, Gary Player, one of the first to start this shadow-boxing on golf greens around the world, employs the clenched fist and the most convincing fresh-air punch in the game. Gary is a master-puncher. Like Gene Tunney, he's won many a championship fight by making a putt and then making a fist of it.

Golfers addicted to clenched-fist celebrations confine their gestures mostly to success on the greens, but here and there one sees more demonstrative players raise 'bunches of fives' aloft as they hit woods and long irons close to the flagsticks. As the gallery cheers a long iron that pulls up a few inches short of the stick, the perpetrator of the shot makes a fist-acknowledgment from a distance. 'Here I am,' he seems to say. 'I'm the guy who did it!'

Yes. Making a fist of it in tournament and championship golf is spreading as fast as runny honey on hot toast. Like the honey, there's no telling where it will end. Will top tournament golfers soon be raising a 'bunch of fives' as they emerge from locker-rooms, step onto the first tee, sign autographs and so on? Will it soon catch on in the interview tents as the players face the Press? A particularly good quote is a matter of celebration.

Mannerisms in sport are noticeably catching. One has only to think of the bouncing of the ball by the server at lawn tennis. Someone started the habit by making one or two bounces. Now every Wimbledon performer does it. And the bounces have increased to the point of monotony. Not just one or two. Not merely three or four. But up to an irritating dozen on every serve! If the server has a 'let' or two, the ball-bouncing adds greatly to the time spent on court. If the bounces continue to increase, the balls will become so worn out that the ball-changes will have to be more often than every seven games.

The popularity of the clenched fist in professional golf suggests that 'bunches of fives' may soon appear on the long-handicap scene. Amateurs invariably imitate professionals, and the outlook is rather worrying. Are we soon to witness the 24-handicapped Rector brandishing a 'bunch of fives' as he sinks a two-foot putt and wins his match on the final green with a hideous 9? And – even more worrying – will the Rector's golfing habits become so ingrained that he will forget where he is and follow a cracking sermon with an unseemly clenched fist from the pulpit? One fears the very etiquette of the game is under threat. Even Lady Captains will need to take a firm grip on their emotions, or they will find themselves screwing up a tight-fisted 'bunch of fives' and punching the air like Seve Ballesteros.

24   In the Warped Mind's Eye

What – in golfing terms – is the meaning of 'in the warped mind's eye'? Well, I can offer no better illustration than to quote big Archie Compston's remark as he stood towering over and about twice the height of a little fellow with a close cropped crew-cut. He rubbed the palm of his hand up and down the fellow's hair and exclaimed: 'Gee, what a lie for a brassie!'

Of course, one way and another, most golfers view the world with a warped eye. Indeed, there are uncounted warped motorists who are quite unable to come upon the road sign 'BEND' without thinking of a slice or hook, or dog-legged hole. Again, the golfer in church is sometimes guilty of irreverence by employing his warped mind's eye in totalling hymn numbers displayed on the board. On observing 343 followed by 232, he says to himself: 'What a pretty start to a scorecard!' Moreover, if he keeps these out-of-place thoughts to himself, who would know of his golfing fantasies in church? Usually, however, his spiritual weakness is brought to an untimely end by the figures of the next hymn, number 599, which puts him out in a miserable 40, instead of an anticipated below-30 score.

Is it possible for the golfer with the warped mind's eye to play golf in bed? No less an authority than Bernard Darwin found it so. In *The Links of Eiderdown* he wrote of enjoying nothing more than feeling just sufficiently unwell to offer a good excuse for spending a day in bed. There, his golf memories and imagination ran riot to such an extent that he continually saw golf links designed on the 'land of the counterpane'. In his warped mind's eye the contours of the eiderdown became undulating golf links which, by frequent changes of his limbs under the bedclothes, he was able to imagine as holes from Formby to Birkdale, Prestwick to Liphook, and so on. Later in the day, when Bernard's tea came in on a tray, to be placed on a bed-table with four legs, the golfing terrain changed from a wholly flat landscape to one that was wooded.

Perhaps at this stage we should pause to wonder whether Darwin was really as well as he thought he was. But since other highly respected writers have used their warped mind's eye in similar fashion, we can assume all was well and that Bernard was up and about again in a day or two.

Scottish historian, poet and journalist Andrew Lang – himself a golfer of the old school – disclosed his warped mind's eye in a parody he wrote of Sir Walter Scott's *Waverley*. The incident he chose to lampoon was that in which Baron Bradwardine quarrelled with a third cousin on his mother's side, Sir Hew Halbert, who had derided his family name by insinuating that the founder of the line had been nothing more important than a 'bear-warden', a custodian of wild beasts. This slur implied that the family's coat of arms had not been achieved by honourable actions in war but simply by a pun upon the family name. The quarrel went unexplained in Scott's novel, the Baron saying no more than, '… that it was settled in a fitting manner.' So, armed with his knowledge of golf and his warped mind's eye, Lang set about an explanation.

The scene for his parody was the Old Course at St Andrews, where, after attending a funeral at the cathedral kirkyard, the Baron and Sir Hew were made to meet at Glass's Inn. There, in the presence of many gentlemen, the two had their unfortunate quarrel, which resulted in a duel the next morning 'on a secluded spot of the sands hard by the town, at the Eden-mouth.' Lang took the trouble to identify this spot as the High Hole, which seems to place the duel and pistol-shooting in the vicinity of the seventh and eleventh holes. In short, the High Hole (Out) and High Hole (Home).

Lang decided on pistols as the chosen weapons, saying that, because of a slight infirmity, Sir Hew was unable to use the sword. The seconds – Inchgrabbit for the Baron and Strathtyrum for Sir Hew – stood by, the pistols were charged and primed, and the two antagonists faced one another at a distance of twelve paces. Word was given to fire and, the pistols having been discharged and the smoke cleared away, Sir Hew was discovered fallen to the ground and senseless with blood flowing freely from a face-wound.

With Sir Hew still unconscious and lying on the ground, a cry of 'Fore!' was heard, but little heed was paid to it because of the urgency of Sir Hew's condition. When he was lifted and his wound examined, closer inspection showed it to be no shot-wound but a knock or bruise, the reason for which soon became apparent. He had been struck by a golf ball driven by a golfer hidden by the dunes and quite unobserved by the duelling party. This assumption was at once confirmed by the sight of a golfer appearing with his clubs, cleeks and irons under his arm. And such was the fellow's concentration on his golf that, without paying the slightest attention to the duelling party, he struck the ball which had felled Sir Hew in the direction of the hole!

The concensus of opinion was that both pistol shots had missed their aim. That Sir Hew had fallen to a chance blow from the golfer's ball. Moreover, as he was still *hors de combat* and incapable of any further action (and quite oblivious of the cause of his condition), the seconds discreetly thought it best that the incident should be kept quiet and that Sir Hew should never be informed of what happened.

Lang's parody was concluded by a statement that Sir Hew wore a bullet among the seals of his watch, he being persuaded by his second that it had been extracted from his brain-pan, which Lang described as the thickest.

In his mind's eye the golfer can dream up any warped incident from the game, true or false, and it must have been a pretty warped mind with a charming sense of humour that reported a golf ball being driven through a window and knocking over a candle that set fire to the room. However, all was not lost. With great presence of mind, the golfer teed another ball, smashed a fire-alarm glass and so summoned the fire brigade ...

25 Acknowledging the Cloth Cap

'I would go back to our house – right by the thirteenth green – and get a cap full of old balls and my mashie and putter and go out to the thirteenth green and pitch them all on and putt them all out, over and over again.'

That was Bobby Jones writing of himself at a very tender age as a budding golfer. Like every schoolboy of the day, he was rarely without his cloth cap, especially on the golf links, and in this instance was filling it with a supply of practice balls to take out to the East Lake, Atlanta, course. Of course the cloth cap in Bobby's day was the most favoured form of headgear on the links. But since then keen competition from other forms of golf caps has been such that the cloth cap is tending to disappear from the scene as suddenly as though snatched off by a zoo monkey. In its place we see the large-peaked cap of baseball origin that makes modern golfers look rather like Donald Duck in spiked shoes.

Earliest golf was played in top hats and caps, with feather and gutty balls. The style of the day was toppers for the gents and caps for the professionals and caddies, who were more or less one and the same. Apart from gracing the noblest heads on the links, the top hat was useful as a measure of the number of feathers required to fill the tiny, stitched leather cases in the making of feather balls. Moreover, in some miraculous way, old-time golfers managed to swing a club and wear a top hat at the same time. One humorous fellow put his top hat to effective use as a means of learning to keep the head still. He concealed a number of small sleighbells inside the hat and trained himself to wear it and strike the ball without ringing the bells.

Golfers also sported the trilby and pork-pie hat and, despite the green pork-pie hat sounding today like an angry complaint to the Public Health Department, both stayed for many years on the golf scene. The trilby was worn by Winston Churchill golfing at Cannes in 1913, while First Lord of the Admiralty, and there are photographs of Henry Cotton in a pork pie at Southport in the thirties. 'Mr Lu', Formosan runner-up to Lee Trevino in the Open at Birkdale, endeared himself to the gallery as he doffed his pork-pie hat with a flourish at exciting moments. The trilby hat topped the swings of Ted Ray, Macdonald Smith, Tommy Armour, Leonard Crawley, Harry Weetman, Sam Snead, Bing Crosby and many others. Even Harry Vardon and Bobby Jones, inveterate wearers of the cloth cap, occasionally wore the trilby. But one can understand why trilbies and pork pies were later confined to their boxes with the lids battened down tight. They were nightmarish to keep on in truly windy conditions. Golfers and caddies, unexpectedly diverted from the fairways by sudden gusts of wind from all quarters, were continually running after hats. As in Chesterton's essay *On Running After One's Hat*, they had to learn to look upon hat-retrieving as a sport in itself and really warm to the chase.

Alongside tall hats, trilbies, panamas, straws, pork pies and homburgs, the discriminating golfer always wore the cloth cap. No other form of headgear comes anywhere near equalling its records and former popularity. Practically all the great champions of the past were cap-wearers. Old Tom Morris's cap was as indispensable as his long white beard. His son, Young Tom, a Glengarry-wearer, waggled his club so violently that his cap often fell from his head in the process. Also, as said earlier, Bobby Jones rarely golfed without his cloth cap. Starting at six years of age, he swung sweetly in a cap, and was still faithful to one when he retired in 1930. His famous Grand Slam (the unique four majors in 1930, when he won the British and American Open and Amateur championships) was captured in a cloth cap. And what of the Triumvirate – Harry Vardon, J.H. Taylor and James Braid? They were seldom seen without their cloth caps. Vardon wore a great big flat one, wide as an outsize frisby, and in one of his instructional books is seen with a fishing line attached to the peak, trying out a device for keeping the head still. To imagine Braid without a cap at his beloved Walton Heath is as sacrilegious as imagining a commissionaire in a cap without braid.

Cloth-cap wearing on the links was not exclusively for

warming British heads. American golfers also favoured this form of headgear. Who in his right mind could think of Ben Hogan without a cloth cap? It was as much a part of his Open victory at Carnoustie as his remarkable three decades in the game. Similarly, Gene Sarazen's cloth cap was as much a part of his golfing personality as his natty knickers. Playing Troon's Postage Stamp in the 1973 Open, at seventy-one years of age, Gene became the oldest competitor in a major championship to hole in one and, on reaching the green, hurriedly put his cap over the hole to stop the ball escaping! Incidentally, the youngest ever to hole in one in the Open was Young Tom Morris, at seventeen the reverse of Sarazen's age, and he too did the feat in a cap.

Arnold Palmer was very much addicted to his cloth cap in the stormiest of weather during his win at Birkdale in 1961, and Bobby Locke's white Palm Beach cap and white shoes are still spoken of in hushed voices in large clubhouses and small artisan huts around the world. Peter Thomson and Tom Watson are five-time cloth-cap winners of the Open, and Gary Player is another cloth-cap more-than-once winner. Of course Harry Bradshaw's cloth cap, worn at a raking angle, is an Irish sartorial classic that no one could match.

Great writers have put pen to paper under cloth caps. Inspired, unmatched prose flowed from under Bernard Darwin's cap, battered and worn though it sometimes seemed, and no golfer could swear at the game more convincingly from under a cap. Horace Hutchinson's essays were capped with the same touch of genius, as were Harold Hilton's, John L. Low's and others. Golf is rich in literature first thought of under cloth caps, often with scribbled notes and pencils parked inside.

One of the greatest of modern golfers, Seve Ballesteros, Open champion on two occasions, has yet to make his appearance in a cloth cap. Such a sight would be as electrifying as seeing a cloth cap on the head of a daring Spanish matador. Bulls ordinarily mesmerized by the matador's cape might be even more mesmerized by a cloth cap. But certainly no lady spectator would agree to Seve's beautiful black hair being hidden by a cloth cap. However, among the young golfers of outstanding ability, Sandy Lyle, Scotland's Open champion of 1985, nobly keeps up the cloth-cap traditions of bygone days.

Perhaps, coupled with Ken Brown's knitted tea-cosy, Norman

von Nida's beret was the most unusual headgear on the links. The little Australian's trademark of a black beret always singled him out from other golfers. Bobby Locke told an amusing story about this, which has since become a favourite with stand-up comedians. He recounted an occasion when von Nida drove out of bounds and landed in a cow pasture. On going into the pasture to recover his ball, von Nida's beret fell off – and Locke said: 'Norman tried on half a dozen different ones before he managed to find his own!'

26   Five Flags on the Green

Doubtless, as a golfing man, you would be singularly surprised and not a little confused to find, as you prepared to play your approach to the green, not *one* but *two* flags in different positions on the green. Moreover, if your golf was of sufficiently high standard to allow you the expectation of pitching somewhere near the flagstick, which flag would you choose? Perhaps, failing some immediate explanation of the two flags (outside double vision caused by a convivial golf-club lunch), you would attempt to hit your approach so that it came to rest midway between flags, and so gave you an option for holing out from the nearest point.

A second flag and additional hole on the green are being proposed by a Dallas businessman who wants to see a six-inch hole as an alternative to the standard 4¼ inch in general use under today's rules. He says: 'We'd just like to see two flags on each green, with one in a six-inch hole to give golfers an option.' He maintains that this would speed up play and make golf 'easier and more fun', and claims that the six-inch hole would eliminate three-putting.

Of course, as any golfing bishop will readily confirm, there's little that's new in golf and gaiters, and this idea of a larger hole was experimented with in America over fifty years ago. In 1933 in Florida, a professional golf tournament was played with an 8½ inch hole on all greens. It was thought it would handicap the good putters and give the not-so-good (but better shot-makers) a greater chance of winning. It didn't work out that way though. Paul Runyan, an acknowledged expert among putters, was the victor and, incidentally, the only competitor who didn't three-putt throughout the tournament. One leading professional had as many as thirteen three-putt greens, and another, Olin Dutra, who was good enough to win the United States Open the following year, had two *four*-putt greens. Over-

confidence seems to have been the players' undoing. With so large a hole, they tended to charge their putts and often finished ten feet past.

In 1968, in their publication *The Search for the Perfect Swing*, the Golf Society of Great Britain conducted an experiment to test the effect of the 8½ inch hole compared with the normal 4¼ inch, and concluded that a scratch man would save something like six shots putting at the larger hole. With the six-inch, the saving would be correspondingly less, and the Society's editors were doubtful of a larger hole making for a better game of golf.

These are some of the answers for the modern-day golfers who look to the larger hole as an antidote to slow play and their putting problems. But what of those golfers, unmentioned so far, who favour a *smaller*, *three*-inch hole and have long practised with it and so believe in it implicitly? 'After practice with the small three-inch hole, the regulation 4¼ inch hole looked as big as a washtub,' said Willie Park, junior, old-time Scottish Open champion. He practised his putting for eight hours a day with a three-inch hole and declared himself stone-dead at two yards. And what of the American, Walter Travis, cigar-smoking 'Old Man', as he was called, stroking the ball with his infamous Schenectady, the centre-shafted putter subsequently banned for forty years by the Royal and Ancient? Here was another master-putter of bygone days who practised with the three-inch hole and, if reference be needed, was said to be able to putt the eyes out of a chipmunk – whatever that may mean. 'Have you seen the American who is putting with an extraordinary thing like a croquet mallet?' asked everyone at Royal St George's, Sandwich, as Travis putted one opponent after another into oblivion on his way to capturing the British Amateur championship, to become the first American winner. So, as you can see, the claims of the smaller hole are well established historically, with authenticated championship successes. Perhaps, then, we can conclude that the three-inch hole is the best of all.

Not so fast! If smaller is better in putting practice, what of Robert Lynd's celebrated jam-pot? As any unwilling assistant knows who has helped out in the jam-making season, the diameter of a jam-pot is only 2⅛ inches, and if we look at it objectively, Lynd's sunken jam-pot may well be the best hole of all.

On his own admission, Robert Lynd, the famous essayist, was no great golfer, merely an enthusiastic putter who competed for the Jam-Pot and String Open Championship over half a century ago. The championship's venue was a lawn at a country house where Lynd was staying. There was a yew at one corner and a cypress opposite, and in the middle of the lawn was a sunken jam-pot, its rim level with the top of the grass. Lynd's opponents in this exciting event were his young nieces and their grandmother who, together with Lynd, went neck-and-neck at the jam-pot, attempting to hole in one. Laid out on the lawn alongside the jam-pot were small circles of string which represented additional golf holes. Lynd wrote that the jam-pot had never been holed in under two strokes: two was the record jointly held by nieces, grandmother and himself. The first time the elder niece did the jam-pot in two, she rushed excitedly into the house shouting: 'Mammy, mammy, I got into the jam-pot in two. I nearly got into it in one, but there was a leaf just at the edge of the jam-pot and ...'

'Golf bore! Golf bore! Go away!' cried her mother. 'I forbid you to play golf until you are twenty-one.'

Never having been conquered in under two strokes, Lynd's jam-pot has obvious merits in its 2⅛ inches, which present an intriguing challenge to golfers as a size of hole for golf greens, no longer to be passed over lightly as suitable only for buttered scones and cream teas. And there's no doubt that, in conjunction with the Dallas businessman's proposal for two holes and flags on each green, we must do our utmost to meet everyone's fancy and provide no fewer than *five* holes and flags, ranging in size from 8½ down to three inches, plus Lynd's 2⅛ jam-pot.

Some sort of multi-coloured flag system would need to be introduced, of course, but flags of four colours could identify the different-sized holes, excluding the jam-pot, which might be at its best sporting a flag bearing the outline of a large raspberry, don't you think?

27 Has-Beens and Never-Wasers

'That was a beautifully struck fourth putt of yours,' said the Has-been to his partner as they moved towards the next teeing-ground. 'If you hadn't sunk it, we'd have lost the hole.'

'Ah, well, you see,' replied the Never-waser, 'I was up at dawn, practising on the bedroom carpet.'

Now, although this was a Has-been congratulating a four-putting Never-waser, it might just as easily have been vice versa, for there's little to choose between them. Each has a foot hovering over the grave with the other scratching about in an unraked bunker. Like pheasants, they go about in braces, and their nether garments are plus-twos. They would refuse to be seen dead in ordinary common-or-garden trousers. Indeed, you can recognize them by their spindleshanks and concertina hose, for no garter has yet been invented that will cohabit with a set of drumsticks.

One such Has-been of our acquaintance is Sam Butterworth, but Sam's also a bit of a Never-waser, too. For more years than we care to think of, the Royal and Ancient game has been Butterworth's disease. Like red corpuscles, he's got it in the bloodstream, and he has arranged to be cremated alongside his favourite Gene Sarazen jigger, balding teddy-bear and confidential copies of *Playboy*. But not yet awhile. Especially now that he believes his drives are getting longer because he's eating raw carrots in abundance.

'The shredded carrot is not only a valuable medicine but also an effective aid to longer driving,' he says.

But everyone knows that Sam Butterworth lost his length years ago and has tried everything, including raw carrots, to get it back. He's had his shafts lengthened, his woods weighted, his grips renewed, but he still can't get up in 3 at the par 4s or 4 at the par 5s. What's more, on eighteen-inch putts, he has a comical habit of twitching the ball five feet past the hole. Observant members declare that when Sam takes a wood from the bag the local magpies and jays hurriedly move in closer on their tree-perches. It's said the birds know from past experience that he'll never achieve lift-off and are rushing for a close-up of the fun.

But Sam thinks he can still reach the woods.

'How are you playing, Sam?' asks a passing member.

'I'm hitting the woods just fine,' says Sam, 'but I'm having a hell of a time getting out of them!'

Apart from deafness and having to bark at one another like seals, Has-beens and Never-wasers become absent-minded. Never-waser Lionel Crackett drives his wife crazy by tunelessly whistling and humming as he pitches into the cat-basket – often with the cat still in it. Or he may rise abruptly from the breakfast table, balancing a sausage on the fork's end, pivoting and trying desperately to pull his stomach back to where John Jacobs says it should be.

'Be careful with that sausage, Lionel,' says his wife.

'Sausage? What sausage?'

'That on the end of your fork. Don't let it fall on the carpet, my dear.'

And Lionel, coming down from his top-of-the-swing reverie, takes a surprised glance at the sausage, eats it up self-consciously and then shuffles off into the garden with his Bobby Jones mashie-niblick.

Lionel's been known to keep his wife awake half the night by describing a shot that finished inches from the pin at the 15th. He once woke her at two in the morning to describe a superlative bunker shot he'd forgotten to mention at dinner.

'Sam Snead calls it a fried-egg lie and tells you to pick up the club more sharply on the backswing,' he shouted into her sleep-bemused ear.

'A fried egg?' she cried, startled out of her wits and suddenly sitting bolt upright in bed. 'What do you want with a fried egg at two in the morning?'

Well, that's Lionel Crackett. A Never-waser without doubt, but also a bit of a Has-been, too. At one time he was an MP. But it was his own fault. He was warned by his headmaster that he'd come to a bad end.

One of Lionel's latest fads is controlling his breathing by Hatha Yoga.

'Does it look like I'm breathing in or out?' he asks his partner.

'Neither, Lionel. The consensus of opinion is that you stopped breathing some time ago.'

Playing the hilliest hole on the course, he asks: 'Do you think I'll make a par?'

'Make a par? With your odd ideas of breathing, you'll be lucky to make the hill.'

Still, it's no good our saying the Has-beens and Never-wasers have bagged their last birdies and should be confined to rocking-chairs to mumble crustily over *The Times* letters and crossword. Providing they can stagger zigzag over the links without tripping too often over the trolley wheels or skewering themselves in tender places on the handle, their golf goes on forever. No one should make the mistake of writing them off the scorecards too soon. The late Harry Weetman once did that to his regret.

Travelling by train, he followed up a long chat about golf with an eighty-year-old stranger with the question: 'Did you play golf, then?'

'What d'you mean, *did* I play golf?' the old chap answered indignantly. 'I do play golf every day, and what's more I mean to play for a long time yet.'

'I was completely silenced,' said Harry.

Harry also recalled a ninety-year-old golfer who was honoured by a Scottish municipal authority by giving him free golf for the rest of his life!

I've often wondered if the old fellow, being a canny Scot, forthwith played thirty-six holes a day, plus a few extra ones during the long summer evenings. After all, at that age, courting can always be left for the darker nights ...

28   Passing Trains of Thought

'There is no joy in the world to equal that of strolling after a London porter who is looking for an empty smoker in which to put your golf clubs,' said A.A. Milne.

Milne was about to leave London for his summer holidays but was uncertain of the best time to go. Being a lover of London life and loath to miss anything that was going on, he decided that it would be best to go away for four separate weeks, instead of taking a whole month at a time. Also, he calculated that if he made such arrangements, he would have the rare joy of strolling after a London porter carrying his golf clubs *four* times instead of only once.

It is all of sixty years since Milne expressed such thoughts, and it's questionable whether the joy he got could be repeated by today's golfer. The thought of a London porter carrying one's golf clubs, let alone finding an empty compartment in which to put them, is rather laughable. Moreover, it seems likely – Government health warnings being what they are – that today's strolling golfer would request the porter (if he could find one) to find him a non-smoker, his doctor having told him that non-smokers are longer off the tee and far less likely to wheeze like old billygoats when the going gets tough. Come to think of it, would today's golfer be *strolling*? The pace of life (in London, in particular) has hotted up so much in sixty years that hardly anyone finds time to stroll any more, least of all down a station platform.

Apart from Milne, if we wish to know how much joy old-time golfers got out of travelling to golf by train, we need look no further than the writings of Bernard Darwin. Train journeys frequently pop in his books, almost always on the way to and from golf, and his railway mood is invariable one of exultation touched with nostalgia.

For example, after taking a cab to Euston – a station he

described as 'most dear and romantic' – Darwin would instruct a
porter to fix a label to his golf bag and, tipping him sixpence for
the trouble, would start his journey alone in a corner seat
(labelled clubs on the luggage rack above his head), watching
the stations whirl by.

Watching the stations whirl by was a favourite pastime of
Darwin's, for he was always on the lookout for golf courses
alongside the track. Travelling from Euston, he would sit at the
window in anticipation of the third hole at Oxhey. From King's
Cross, he looked out for Royston Heath. But Waterloo afforded
the richest feast of all by giving him glimpses of Esher, Byfleet,
Woking, West Hill and Bramshot. The short 7th at Woking was
close to the line, with glimpses of the fifth green and fourth
fairway.

Brief glimpses of these courses were exciting enough for Darwin, but a greater thrill was to see someone playing a stroke – preferably a *bad* one – so that, being alone in the compartment, he could jeer without anyone knowing. Sometimes, however, he felt cheated by the train's being just too early or late to witness the execution of a stroke, or by a golfer waggling so long over the ball that the train snatched the scene away before the swing got under way.

In reading Darwin, I find myself worrying over those clubs balanced on the luggage rack above his head. Transporting a bag of clubs in that manner must have been a hazardous business. Admittedly, bags of clubs were much smaller in the old days, but so were luggage racks. Golf wasn't a popular and well-known sport in Darwin's early days, and one can imagine non-golfers entering the compartment, heavily laden with bundles and baskets (and Uncle Albert's parrot in its cage) and finding nowhere to put them – and all because some great big fellow, dressed in knickbockers, was travelling by train to play a silly game!

'I think, sir, you should have put your weapons [weapons!] in the guard's van. They're far too cumbersome for a luggage rack; and, if I may make so bold, distinctly dangerous to be stowed above one's head.'

If those early days of golf didn't elicit criticism of this kind from difficult passengers, there was always the affable nincompoop, I suppose, who pointed to the bag above one's head and said: 'Been 'aving a bit o' crokey, Mister?'

Not keeping his clubs with him in the compartment would have been unthinkable for Darwin, who tells us that he liked to keep looking up at them over his head in anticipation of the golfing pleasures to come, as well as to assure himself that they were actually there, and not left behind on Euston station. Also, if he was travelling with other golfers, the clubs on the rack were a source of continual amusement and speculation, for he and his companions were not averse to trying out one another's favourite clubs in the confined space of the carriage. Though Bernard doesn't say as much, I think we can assume that no non-golfers were among the fellow-passengers when such antics took place. Waggling someone's unfamiliar niblick and cracking an old lady on the shin was certainly not Darwin's style.

Train travel today compares unfavourably with that romantic era, of which Darwin said: 'There is something of old enchantment in the memory that we got cheap blue tickets for half-a-crown and no more, and travelled in dear, varnished second-class carriages with red cushions.'

How's that for the age of the train? Varnished carriages with red cushions! And only second class, at that!

Whenever I reflect on golfers journeying by train to play golf, I am reminded of Bing Crosby catching the early train from London's Liverpool Street station to go golfing with that celebrated journalist Pat Ward-Thomas, by whom he was invited to play on the writer's home course of Brancaster in Norfolk. Bing arrived at Downham Market carrying only driver and spoon in a light case. No battery of irons in an immense bag. Just two favourite wooden clubs, as the easiest of luggage to pop up on the rack.

I like to think that Bing travelled alone and, like Darwin and companions, took down from the luggage rack both driver and spoon to waggle them appreciatively a few times in anticipation of the fine golf to come on Brancaster links. Two clubs on the rack in a light case would be easily got at, rather than zipped up tight in a whacking great bag. As I say, if he was lucky enough to travel alone, I can't imagine his resisting the temptation.

But there's another, less fanciful, passing train of thought that I cherish for that Brancaster journey. It's a *smoking* compartment – to provide for the briar pipe that always peeped out from Bing's top pocket …

29 Plumb-Bobbing on the Line

Reading the greens is as tricky a job as attempting to pick out a perfect cabbage in the greengrocer's. There are days when we read them as easily as the pages of a well-known author. But, inexplicably, there are those when we fail to pick out a single line. It's then that, in desperation, we may ask ourselves about the art of plumb-bobbing.

Is there much to recommend it? Many great golfers who perform skilfully on the greens question its usefulness. They never use it. They pick out the line by standing or squatting behind the ball and looking towards the hole with both eyes open, instead of closing one and dangling the putting-stick between finger and thumb at arm's length, like tempting a cat with a tail-hung mouse and winking at it at the same time. Or – if you think the simile inappropriate – like the late Lord Castlerosse disdainfully holding out a dripping umbrella and instructing his caddie to have it destroyed.

Of course, before you can squint along the line with confidence, there's this business of finding one's master eye. The right eye for the right-hander, and vice versa. But, as there are exceptions to this rule, you can settle the question by a simple test. Select an object some fifteen feet away about the size of your fist (the bartender's nose will do). Point at his nose with your right index finger. Then close one eye. If you seem still to be pointing directly at his nose, it's your master eye that's open. Close your master eye and open the other, it will appear that his nose has moved a few inches to one side. If he should give you a queer look, order another drink quickly, pretending that's what you were on about.

The master eye does the lining up to the ball and then on to the hole. The other eye must be kept closed. But is it sensible to

select the line of putt with one eye closed, and then putt with both eyes open? In the interests of not missing anything (much can be missed with only one eye open), aren't two peepers better than one? Who can say? Would the Royal and Ancient clubhouse have fallen down if the surveyor had plumbed it with both eyes instead of only one behind his instruments?

Sometimes confusion enters into the plumb-bobbing art. Absent-minded golfers tend to forget which eye they're supposed to close, and which keep open. And if, by some minor golfing miracle, they remember correctly, they sometimes forget the significance of the ball appearing left or right of the putter-shaft. 'If the putter-shaft falls to the left of the hole, the putt will break from left to right,' they say to themselves quietly so that no one will hear. 'If the shaft falls to the right, the putt will break from right to left.' Is that right, or should it be the opposite? They would like to check the details again, but they haven't got the damned book. And everyone's staring and telling them to get on with it in the gathering dusk.

Even if the golfer has carried out the plumb-bobbing art to perfection, the question arises as to how much borrow should be allowed for on whichever side it appears to be. Experts say this is largely a matter of experience, but other considerations enter into it as well. Some advocates of the system tell us that it's recommended mainly for use near mountains and the sea. 'On mountain courses in particular, optical illusions can play tricks. The green may seem perfectly level when you are standing on it, but actually it will nearly always be sloping away from the nearest mountain.' Similarly, greens on seaside links almost always slope towards the sea. I guess it's a bit like the Hoylake golfer who said: 'How the blazes can a chap hope to read the line with such a ghastly smell of sea air about?'

Recently a golfer wrote to me and asked if I thought a monocle would help him to pick out the correct line. I gathered that his master eye was lagging lamentably behind the other, but I doubted if a monocle would help. There's not much call for monocles these days, perhaps because they were always dropping into plates of porridge and beermugs and had to be removed (from the eye, not the porridge and beermugs) in order to blow one's nose. Losing a monocle on the golf course in rough or heather would cause a sticky problem, like dropping one's contact lens in the marmalade. In all my years of golf I've never seen a monocle used, but James Agate, journalist and author and first-rate amateur golfer, declared that a monocle was responsible for his winning a massive silver ink-well in the men's foursomes of a North of England golf tournament. After a gruelling match, with the sides all square, both were on the last green in two. Agate ran his approach putt two yards past the hole. His opponents putted up to within a foot. Agate's partner bravely holed and, just as the foot putt was about to be conceded by Agate, said: 'Wait a bit, I think I'll see that in.' And he took from his pocket a monocle, which Agate did not know him to possess, fixed it in place and concentrated all his attention on the tin. 'Our opponents said it wasn't fair. It wasn't. But Man has to get on in this world as best he can,' said Agate.

Another Agate story, which I can't resist telling, though it has nothing to do with golf, concerned a young English subaltern, attached to an Australian regiment, who was in the habit of coming on parade wearing a monocle. One morning every Aussie in his troop had his identity-disc fixed in his eye. The subaltern threw his eye-glass up in the air and caught it again in his cheek. 'Do that, you blighters!' he said.

A golfer's success in reading the greens depends on what he sees. Maybe I'm wrong, but I can't recall Bobby Locke relying on plumb-bobbing. Yet he saw everything. Every undulation, every bit of grit, the way the grass grew, the way the whole was cut and, every bit as important, *the way the wind blew*. He was – as Chesterton said of a different subject – an ocular athlete. He didn't let the eye rest. 'Why should the eye be lazy?' asked Chesterton. 'Let us exercise it until it learns to see the startling facts that run across the landscape as plain as a painted fence. Let us learn to write essays on a stray cat or a coloured cloud.'

On that note I will end, except to say that, apart from looking very impressive and attractive while plumb-bobbing her way to success on the greens, Nancy Lopez always seemed to be winking at me ...

30   Straight from the
Harbour's Mouth

Let us consider golfing in hotel bedrooms. Let us suppose that, because of incessant rain and the unfitness of the course, you were confined to your room and at rather a loss to know how to while away the time. What would you do? Perhaps take up your putter and work for an hour or so at stroking putts over the bedroom carpet. Or, being a chap of a more daring and adventurous turn of mind, you might swing your wedge, remove the odd divot or two from the bedroom rugs, attempt to pitch into the wash-hand basin or maybe give the antique furnishings what is known in the trade as a 'distressed finish'.

But hold on. If your hotel room overlooked the harbour, instead of merely pussyfooting around with putter and wedge, would you open wide the window and, taking a resolute grip on your driver, whack a few experimental shots into the water?

I doubt it, Cyril. Wouldn't you fear mis-hitting the ball so that, remaining indoors instead of proceeding rapidly into the harbour, it zigzagged alarmingly round and round the room like a furious bluebottle, richocheting off walls and ceiling and leaving a trail of destruction in its path?

'Would you mind explaining it, sir? Tell me what happened.'

That's the hotel manager speaking to you.

'Well, you see, I was driving a ball out of the open window into the harbour, and I'm afraid the damage to the room was caused by a faulty wrist-break and incorrect follow-through. What can I do to make amends?'

The hotel manager fixes you with his steely eye, takes hold of the offending club and says: 'Why don't you try holding the club like this, sir, and letting the follow-through take care of itself?'

Most hotel managers – like mental nurses – are familiar with odd behaviour, particularly that of dedicated golfers. Their chambermaids have reported tartan plus-twos left under the mattress, tumblers on the carpet and tee-pegs in the wastepipes and toilet. Lucky rabbit-paws and even luckier unwashed socks are frequently removed from inside pillow-cases. Every tournament has its aftermath of dog-eared scorecards and swing-tips secreted inside hotel literature and Bibles.

Of course, as you may already have guessed, these jottings on golf in hotel bedrooms arise from a report of Greg Norman hitting a hundred balls through the open window of his hotel room into Hong Kong harbour. Bored stiff by being unable to play golf because the first two rounds of the Hong Kong Open Championship were washed out by rain, and doubtless feeling as restricted as a goldfish in a bowl, he hit out at convention and bombarded the harbour with a hundred balls.

Ben Hogan's fellow-professionals tried to avoid getting the hotel room next to his if they could, because in the evenings there was the constant thump-thump of balls putted across the carpet. He said: 'I've been taking a putter back to my hotel room during tournaments for years and have found it worthwhile.'

There's a story of Hogan teamed up with Sarazen – and 8 up at lunch. Gene suggested there was no need to push themselves, they could afford to take it easy. 'I should say not,' said Ben. 'We ought to keep piling it on. If we can beat these guys 14 and 12, I'd like that. I want to get the match over quickly and get back to my room to practice my putting.'

Greg Norman's performance from the hotel window in Hong Kong reminds me of Lord Castlerosse practising his golf swing before an open hotel window in London, but with a few differences. First, Castlerosse was not hitting balls into the Thames, but merely swinging. Secondly, he was going against medical advice, for he was being nursed and in serious ill-health at the time; and, thirdly, the noble Lord was stark naked!

Of course, stories of Castlerosse's frustrations with golf are legendary. Henry Longhurst wrote about an occasion at Walton Heath when Castlerosse had the misfortune to top shot after shot.

'At the last hole he tried a final stroke, with the same result. He tossed the club disdainfully to the ground and stalked towards the clubhouse, uttering the memorable instructions, "Pick that up. Have the clubs destroyed, and leave the course." '

Castlerosse liked a drink of whisky on the course. He insisted on being accompanied by a servant bearing a jug of whisky from which he frequently filled and emptied his glass. Also, at Killarney, his ancestral home, he arranged for a number of huts about the course, to which he held the key. In each was a good supply of whisky.

Another eccentric who believed in a drop of whisky whilst golfing was the famous American comedian W.C. Fields. But in his case, it was drunk secretly, for he'd been recommended to play golf as a *cure* for drinking. Indeed, the doctor who advised the cure even went so far as to play with Fields and insist on checking his breath on the first tee.

'All sober?' he asked Fields. 'Let me smell your breath. OK, then. Off we go. This is the life!'

But though Fields had got the doctor's approval of sobriety at the start of the round, what he'd secreted inside his large golf bag soon changed that. A dozen or so miniature bottles of whisky (which the comedian drank furtively in conjunction with tee-shots into the woods and out-of-the-way sand-traps) soon enabled him to raise his spirits and golf game. As the bottles emptied, his game sharpened up impressively.

'By gad, this golf's doing the trick, Doc.'

And by the end of the round, Fields had won enough money in sidebets to take care of both doctor's fees and the following day's whisky.

31   James Braid and the
Big Drum

'Sam, be quiet,' said Mr Pickwick.

'Dumb as a drum vith a hole in it,' replied Sam.

Now, one doesn't find any golf in *Pickwick Papers*, but that brief dialogue between Mr Pickwick and Sam Weller brings to mind a remarkable iron shot played many years ago by the celebrated Scottish champion James Braid. He had a reputation as a superb iron player and, as I propose to show later, a delightful sense of humour. Both of these attributes have a bearing on my story but, before I talk about Braid's unusual shot, I must first talk of brass bands.

It is a strange thought, I admit, but there used to be military and brass bands at golf matches, and present-day golfers who are put off by the cooing of wood-pigeons and the heavy breathing of earwigs can consider themselves lucky that they're not having to play their shots whilst a brass band performs comic-opera tunes.

Early this century, the brass band was a commonplace sight and sound at sporting events. At cricket matches and festivals, the music played as the game progressed. Jack Fingleton, Australian cricket writer, tells us of bands at test matches in Sydney right up to 1931, when the Springbok captain, Jock Cameron, asked the band not to play as he 'couldn't concentrate while music was in the air'.

This combining of comic-opera tunes and stirring marches with the 'pock' of ball against bat led one poetic writer, Ralph Wotherspoon, to suggest the playing of suitable tunes to meet the game's fluctuations. For instance, he thought it might be a good idea for the band to play the batsman in and out on his solitary walk between pavilion and wicket and vice versa:

The band might play the batsman in,
That stirring march from 'Lohengrin'
Would fill the bill; now how about
A tune to play the batsman out?
No difficulty here at all,
Handel's C Major March in 'Saul'.

No doubt music-loving golfers will have their own ideas of suitable tunes for golf, but 'Colonel Bogey' might be hard to improve on as a curtain-raiser for marching along the first fairway. The tune originated on the golf course, for the composer of this famous march got his inspiration while playing golf. Instead of shouting 'Fore!', an approaching golfer whistled a couple of notes at him and, replying with whistled notes of his own, the composer unexpectedly got the main theme.

Brass bands can be found in Harry Vardon's memoirs, too. When he was the professional at Bury (one of the strongholds of brass bands), he and other golfers had to share the eighteenth green with the Besses-o'-the-Barn Brass Band, who had permission to use the last green as a practice platform on summer evenings.

James Braid was one of four famous golfers engaged to open a south-east course before the First World War, and a full military band played along with them to mark the event.

On their morning round, the professionals went off to various lilts, and one of them complained that he found it difficult to time his shots and demonstrate the finer points of golf to the air of 'Annie Laurie'. He said the tune made him swing much too slowly.

At the last hole of the afternoon round, the brass band was still playing briskly from a position a little to the right of the eighteenth green. This was a rare chance for James Braid to demonstrate the accuracy of his iron play and his great sense of what the Scots call 'pawky' humour.

Golf-writer on the scene R. Endersby Howard said: 'Only a short iron was required from the tee, and I am sure I detected a mischievous gleam in the eye of James Braid as he took the honour. He hit the shot perfectly. It went right through the big drum – such a resounding thwack as that drum had never known before. The band did not wait to see who was coming next. It put its instruments under its arms and fled.'

In all the flurry and excitement of Braid's shot, R. Endersby Howard failed to say what happened to the ball. Did it stay inside the drum and thus create golf's most bizarre hole in one? Or did it burst right through and out the other side and so remain playable, being, so to speak, a rub of the drum? Furthermore, did James get his 3 – or had he to play again from the tee because the drummer ran off with the ball?

Alas, such moments are few, and the magical occasion often passes without proper recognition and appreciation. One can't help thinking that the band's unfavourable reaction to Braid's once-in-a-lifetime shot was comparable only with that of the spoil-sport lady who resented being struck on the head by a cricket ball hit magnificently out of Lord's ...

32   Reported Missing

As a distinct contrast to winning the Masters at Augusta for the second time, Seve Ballesteros added a breath of fresh air to the Italian Open by missing the ball completely and registering an air shot. I don't know what you feel about this, but I noted the rarity appreciatively, seeing it as an encouraging sign for long-handicappers struggling desperately with the game. In short, if Seve can miss the ball completely, there's hope for those who are still hitting it!

Of course, there were extenuating circumstances. Seve's pitch to the green came to rest against an out-of-bounds hedge and, when he tried to chop the ball clear, he failed to make contact. Which brings me to the question – Is the air shot the most humiliating in all golf?

I noticed the other day that the former middleweight boxing champion of the world, Alan Minter, a recent convert to golf, had been saying that his air shots cause him most embarrassment, particularly in pro-celebrity events. I gather that, first off in a pro-celebrity event at Mannings Heath Golf Club, he missed the ball completely and was very relieved that – the hour being 7.45 a.m. – there was hardly anyone about to tut-tut at the curtain-raiser. Anyway, as I see it, at the time of day when only yawning owls are watching, missing the tee-shot is perhaps more commonplace than hitting it.

However, Alan needn't have worried. Missing the ball isn't solely for beginners. They're pretty well versed in the art, it's true, but more than one great champion has suffered the ignominy of attempting to move the ball along, only to find it staying put.

I have a vivid recollection of the great American Lawson Little playing an air shot in a British championship; and certainly,the incomparable Harry Vardon once played one (or should I say *missed* one?) in the US Open, in 1900, which he won by two

strokes from J.H. Taylor. In Harry's case it was sheer careless-
ness. A six-inch tap-in was missed completely.

Betty Jameson, a former US champion, did much the same as
Vardon. Playing in a tournament at Wentworth in 1951, she tried
to tap a tiny putt into the hole back-handed but hit the ground
and missed the ball.

Much more recently, in the 1983 Open at Royal Birkdale, the
former US Open champion Hale Irwin played a dramatic air shot
in the third round. Trying to tap in a two-inch putt on the
fourteenth green, he missed the ball completely, whilst still a very
serious challenger for the title. At the end of the championship,
he was denied a play-off with Tom Watson by only one stroke. He
described his air shot as the costliest miss of his entire career.

Such humiliating moments make golfers profoundly miserable, more especially if they allow their minds to dwell on the extra
stroke on the score-card, but they symbolize the need to treat the
two-inch shot as seriously as the 200-yarder. They also require
the golfer to accept his misfortune philosophically, and concentrate on the job in hand.

If it's true that the air shot is the most humiliating in golf, it's
equally true that the first tee is the most embarrassing place to
play it. First-tee nerves doubtless account for a higher proportion
of air shots than elsewhere, and I once knew a man so badly
affected by them that he carried a nine-inch square of plywood
with a figure 2 painted boldly on it, which he made a habit of
propping against the first tee-box.

Enid Wilson, one of the greatest lady champions of all time,
tells a story embracing both the first tee and an air shot.

'There is a story of an incident that happened on the first tee of
a fashionable seaside course on the Continent. At the height of
the season there was always a crowd awaiting the starter's
pleasure. One day, a moderate woman golfer was stricken with
exceeding fright when she saw that a reigning monarch was in
the crowd. When her name was called, she did what most people
do when they are apprehensive – she hurried and in her panic
missed the ball altogether. A deadly hush ensued. When she
realized what had happened, her wits returned and, with great
presence of mind, she turned to her caddie and remarked in a
peevish voice, as though he was to blame for her mishap: "How
can I be expected to hit the ball when I do not know the length of
the hole?" '

At first sight, the air shot may seem humiliating beyond compare. But Spiro Agnew, ex-Vice-President of the United States, had a rare talent for playing shots even more upsetting to a golfer's reputation. For – I ask you – would you not find it more humiliating to bounce one of your wooden-club shots off the head of a famous professional in the Bob Hope Desert Classic than to play a simple, inoffensive air shot? The head belonged to Doug Sanders, and Spiro Agnew's ball bounced off it in the 1970 Desert Classic.

So feared was the Vice-President's reputation in pro-celebrity events that the ticket-buying public were said to prefer first-tee seats in the *back* – rather than the *front* – row. Spiro sprayed his tee-shots into the gallery at such close quarters that anything could happen – and usually did. Some wag gave the Vice-President the title of 'Slice-President of the United States', and Johnny Carson said that, if ever enemies from outer space invaded the planet, the only defence needed would be the Slice-President attacking them with a 3-wood and a bucket of balls.

But Spiro Agnew always made amends very properly by personally checking for damage to life and limb. On one occasion, having had the misfortune to whack a lady on the ankle from close range, he sent her and her husband on a week's vacation to the Doral Hotel, Miami, with all expenses paid.

Those were the days when White House golfers were in the news. President Eisenhower was once hit by a ball whilst playing in a foursome at Denver's Cherry Hills Country Club in 1954. The golfer who hit him was Maurie Luxford, the man said to have invented celebrity golf, who was known throughout the United States as 'Mr Golf'.

Luxford's shanked shot hit the President with a thud and, terribly humiliated and fearful for the President, he rushed over to Ike and said: 'Mr President, are you hurt?'

Eisenhower pulled a wallet out of his pocket and held it up. 'Maurie,' he said, beaming an infectious grin, 'your ball hit me right in this wallet and that's the only time in my life I've been hit in the pocketbook when it didn't hurt.'

33 All in the Balance

If you care to amuse yourself with a bit of golf that's different, try a Spanish trick or two from the Seve Ballesteros repertoire. For example, for starters, have a go at becoming adept at bouncing a golf ball on the face of an iron or putter. You may see Seve amusing himself in this way in practice rounds, tapping the ball up off the face of an iron as easily as you and I might do it with a table-tennis bat and ball. At first sight, Seve's trick may seem only a passing amusement, but there's more to it than you would think, for it can play a vital part in improving a golfer's touch and feel of the ball. Moreover, Ballesteros isn't the only champion golfer to enliven the game with this little trick. Many professionals are the cat's whiskers at it and, though you may not know it, ball-bouncing has its place in golf's history. Big Ted Ray, former British and US Open champion, declared that it improved his putting touch beyond measure. He said it gave him a better understanding of the weight of the ball, and Ted was so expert that he was able to bounce the ball to varying heights off the putter-face and keep it going like a skilled juggler.

Another of Seve's antics is the balancing of one ball on top of another. This is a whole ball-game more difficult, so you'll need to be cold sober with a pulse as steady as an eight-day clock. Simply hold a golf ball between finger and thumb and, extending it to arm's length, balance another ball on top of it. However, if there's the merest whisper of a breeze about, defer your attempt. But when – and if – you get the knack, Jack, you'll impress everyone with your outward display of self-control.

Johnny Miller says he saw Seve do this trick on the first tee in a professional tournament in which he was leading the field, and adds: 'It shows how steady Seve's nerve is when even the act of balancing a ball on a tee-peg stuck in the ground can cause others unexpected difficulties.'

Ballesteros also has fun putting between his legs and playing bunker shots while standing on one leg, but I don't think you should follow suit, unless you don't mind being carted off in an ambulance and ending up in a hospital bed still wearing your peaked cap and spiked shoes. It's as well to accept that with some tricks – as they said of the solitary pupil in a remote village school – Seve's in a class of his own.

All this talk of balancing tricks makes me think of the chap who took it into his head to balance a heavy golf umbrella on his nose for 2½ hours, apparently with the intention of getting himself (and golf umbrella) into the *Guinness Book of Records*. One wonders why he chose a golf umbrella and what reason he had for treating his nose so disrespectfully. Rough usage of noses is usually confined to boxing rings and rugby scrums and Maori greetings, and balancing an umbrella on the nose for as long as 2½ hours must be exceptionally hazardous. I mean, a sudden sneeze – or, like Edward Lear's Uncle Arly, a stray cricket alighting on the nose – and the whole trick would collapse, perchance with a golf umbrella banged in the eye or wedged unexpectedly in the throat. However, so far as we're able, let's try putting the fellow's performance into some sort of golfing perspective.

In balancing a golf umbrella on the nose, the head must be thrust back as though looking at a fly walking on the ceiling. Of course, to experienced golfers who have missed countless short putts, this is an all-too-familiar pose. Tournament pros adopt it all the time. When a tiddler slips past the hole, they look up accusingly at the heavens and blame Providence. Amateur golfers, too, make tragic gestures at the sky, heads tossed back disdainfully, and even bishops at golf have been known to make quick – but nevertheless significant – upward glances.

Maybe it was this eyes-on-the-heavens pose that gave the chap the nose-balancing idea in the first place. As Mark Twain said, one can see it all through a glass eye darkly. A six-incher having been missed in the pouring rain, the chap's head was thrust back, and up went the umbrella on the end of his nose! Embarrassment really. And it might never have happened if he had stood with bowed head and it had not been raining at the time.

One imagines this umbrella-balancing took place indoors. Outdoor performances would not be feasible. A sudden gust of wind or the inconsiderateness of passing seagulls would be upsetting. Also, chaps with stiff necks are ruled out from the start. But an interesting sidelight is that, in having to keep the nose perfectly still, it teaches the golfer to keep the head still, not only for the few seconds required in executing the golf swing but for 2½ hours on the trot.

Although I do my best to disbelieve what my senses tell me, the possibility that *promotional* golf umbrellas will be nose-balanced in the future, with the various makers competing with one another for the services of the top-notch nose-balancers in the game, is not without interest. If so, we may soon have the advertisement urging us to buy 'The golf umbrella that balances longest on parts that other umbrellas do not reach'.

Let me finish with a word of warning, even to the civilized minds of golf wherein caution is supposed to rule all impulse. Over-indulgence in balancing heavy golf umbrellas may lead to a condition known as 'nose-spread'. Permanent disfiguration may occur, and it's as well to bear in mind Robert Lynd's story of large and unshapely noses. It concerned a man who had such an enormous nose that his friends, on meeting him, used to ask: 'How are you both?'

34 In Search of Utopia

'Tell me about Toad Hall,' said the gaoler's daughter. 'It sounds beautiful.'

'Toad Hall,' said Mr Toad proudly, 'is an eligible self-contained gentleman's residence, very unique; dating in part from the fourteenth century, but replete with every modern convenience. Up-to-date sanitation. Five minutes from church, post office and golf links ...'

Readers of *The Wind in the Willows* will recall Mr Toad as a terror of a motorist, before whom all must give way or be smitten into nothingness and everlasting night, and one hesitates to think of him as a golfer. But Toad Hall – being only five minutes from the golf links – has obvious claims as a possible contender for the Utopian golf residence.

If you're wondering what brings on these dreams of a Utopian golf residence, I must refer you to a letter to the editor of *Golf Monthly* from Keith J. Baines of Lake Worth, Florida, who is searching for the ideal golf house. A Britisher intending to return home after twenty years in the States, he writes: 'I have always dreamt of a house on a hillside overlooking the sea close to a fine links course or courses with great greens, extensive practice facilities ... within walking distance ... no further than a few miles from a good-sized town where there is a theatre or two and the local restaurants could compete with any in the country.' In his appeal for help, Mr Baines asks readers to contact him if they know of the perfect house and promises to follow up all suitable replies.

Incidentally, as a result of the publication of his letter, it was reported that 623 golfing house agents were involved in traffic accidents by rushing blindly to the post office ...

Mr Baines makes no mention of purchase price, so we can let our golfing imaginations run riot, which is exactly what happened in the pages of an old, dog-eared golf book which I now take down from my cobwebby shelves.

It's rather an odd coincidence that this tattered old volume – Henry Leach's *Letters of a Modern Golfer to his Grandfather* – published as long ago as 1910, also envisages the Utopian golf residence, again without reference to the cost involved. However, in this instance, it was a dream not of a single golfer but of a group of at least eight, whose declared purpose in life (apart from playing a couple of rounds of golf a day) was to assist their golfing friend (Herbert Watson, Esq.) to build the Utopian golf residence.

'There was a trifle of difficulty at the beginning in discovering what exactly it was that Herbert wanted. All that he could tell us was that it must be golflike, and must please his most golfing friends and make them realize that they were utterly and completely at home when they were under his roof. It must seem to them that they were in the clubhouse.'

A jolly good chap, Herbert Watson, don't you think? We could use a few like him today, especially as he seems to have been positively loaded with the filthy stuff. Money being no object.

Not surprisingly, the lads went to it with a will. They agreed to form a Committee of Investigation to find out precisely the needs of Herb and his friends, and the committee, after seventeen sittings at its Regent's Park headquarters (Herb's house!), issued an interim report consisting of a few notes on the back of half a sheet of notepaper (doubtless Herb's notepaper), mainly for the guidance of the architect.

'The house will be far out in the country. It will be built in a corner part of some forty acres of land belonging to it, so that it may be near to the first teeing ground and the last green of a private nine-hole course that will be made by Mr Watson at great expense. There will be a small putting course in the gardens surrounding the house, and some driving alleys, down which a man may drive golf balls for a distance of about 150 yards, so that he may know whether he did really slice or pull, top or get under, while a clock arrangement at the end of each alley will indicate the probable length of each drive.'

Leaving nothing to chance, Herb's friends formed several committees. A Committee of Hazards dealt with bunkering. A Course and Lands Committee was responsible for all out-of-doors arrangements. A Rooms and Fitments Committee –

remembering that Herb was desirous of keeping up the standard of his game during inclement weather – strongly recommended the provision of a Swinging Room, where drives could be practised against a padded wall. They also recommended a lofty Pitching Room, where mashie and niblick shots could be experimented with on a matting-laid floor. One of Herb's friends, it seems, ordered a new mat for his front door every month, because he used them up so quickly!

An armoury was proposed where Herb could keep all his clubs on racks. 'Those in use, the spares, the abandoned, the mementos and so forth, not all tumbled away in a corner or in some dark cupboard as they are now at the Villa Watson.' And, as expected of the proposers, there were to be separate sections of the armoury for the convenience of Mr Watson's friends.

The aforesaid friends thought there should also be something in the nature of a professional's shop with a small furnace arrangement in it. They said: 'One of the most entertaining occupations for a wet day is heating the heads of irons and altering the lie and angle of loft thereon, or, if time is rather short, letting a little lead into the sole of drivers, always providing that they are spare or other people's clubs that are experimented with.'

A Dining and Sleeping Committee proposed individual bedrooms for all Herb's friends, containing washbasins with hot and cold water laid on, as in the best dormy houses. And a new idea – a tap of soda water always kept at full charge – was recommended to be let into the wall, architect to be consulted. Telephonic communication between all the bedrooms of the playing members of the house party was thought to be essential, and additional telephones between each room and the groundsman's cabin were to be installed, 'so that proper enquiries as to the weather may be made before rising, particularly on mornings when it is doubtful'.

Other findings of the Dining and Sleeping Committee were that there should be space in each bedroom to swing a club, bathrooms for all, drying rooms and, of course, rooms for billiards and cards.

A Drinks and Smokes Committee gave the utmost attention to the examination of detail in their particular subjects, and even called many witnesses, including wine and cigar merchants. A bar was to be established, drinks to be paid for and the money put in a box and then spent on the purchase of golf balls, which would be dealt out weekly to the members of the party, the arrangements being that those who used the bar most would get most balls. Herbert was to buy the liquids, of course, but members of the various committees felt they could ask him at any time to join them in the friendliest way.

After reading strenuously through all these proposals in Leach's book and being convinced that the Utopian golf residence was there for the taking, I came upon a single snag, hindrance, pitfall, hornet's nest – call it what you will.

The report ended by stating: 'Of course, we have no doubt that Mrs Watson will have some suggestions to make.'

As you may have suspected already, chaps, that's Herb's wife – and the point where we fold our tents, like the Arabs, and as silently steal away ...

35   *Out of the Cradle*

'In a poll to find the best "up-and-down player" of the present day, Seve Ballesteros would win the prize for me as the best stroke-saver around. He is so creative because he learned to play the game as a young boy with only one club and he had to work out how to play all kinds of shots with that rusty old 3-iron and he is reaping the benefits now.'

That statement came from Henry Cotton, and I'm sure a great many golfers will agree with him. To my mind, there's not the slightest doubt that, learning the game as a boy golfer in Pedrena, Seve's wizardry and sureness of touch came into being. But – leaving Seve aside for a moment – is it not written in golf's long history that learning the game as a boy – with all a young boy's inventiveness – is the surest way to golfing greatness? As I've read the autobiographies of champions, this profound and far-reaching truth has repeatedly been evident and, as my readers doubtless recall, I have frequently expressed it. Let me try to prove the point here.

Let me begin with the great Bobby Locke sitting in his perambulator. I'm sure he won't mind, for I do so to emphasize that, if you want to become a champion golfer, you can't take up the game too soon.

Of course, as many of us know, Bobby is said to have played with a golf ball in his pram, and I doubt whether you could find a better illustration of early one-upmanship from the very depths of the cradle, unless you happened to be born in the clubhouse overlooking the first tee, as Laddie Lucas, ex-fighter pilot in the Royal Air Force and former Walker Cup captain, was, and writes about in his book, *The Sport of Princes*.

Lucas writes nostalgically of growing up with local boy caddies. He enjoyed nothing better than playing with them with cut-down irons on an improvised course of three or four holes in front of the pro's shop, later to become a car-park.

He gives us a charming insight into the way in which these young lads developed their game, by saying: 'Bare, grassless lies held no terror for us, chipping the ball into the next sunken tin can. It was a taxing classroom in which to learn the first, rudimentary arts of the game.' The sight of small boys nipping old balls off mud around the back of the pro's shop is one of the lost wonders of the game, says Lucas, and I wholeheartedly agree. It was the training-ground of champions. The cradle of the game.

I don't know whether Bobby Locke's golf-ball juggling in his pram is true. But, if it is, you've certainly got to hand it to him as a pretty shrewd way of getting an early feel for the game ahead of the rest of the fellows!

Most youngsters are greatly influenced by childhood and the first few years of their lives, and these years are particularly important in the game of golf and the imaginative shaping of the swing.

The wee laddies of St Andrews watched and copied the Old Course golfers over a hundred years ago. This is the ideal way to start, watching good players, for youngsters have an inborn gift of mimicry and a natural desire to beat balls around uninhibitedly.

St Andrews lads of the nineteenth century – as enthusiastic as any in the game's history – were sadly lacking in equipment, for they possessed neither clubs nor balls and therefore had to improvise in a unique way. In place of clubs, they used shinty sticks – rather like hockey sticks – and in place of balls, nail-weighted champagne corks, which they collected from rubbish heaps behind the St Andrews hotel and also the Royal and Ancient Club itself. Champagne ran more freely then, so corks were unlimited. The lads drove a nail into each cork to add weight.

These little boys of only seven or eight years, who had no links to play on, played in the streets, in the yellow lamplight of St Andrews. They holed out by striking the lamp-posts with the corks, and were so good they often holed out in 3 on a fifty-yard stretch.

Artful little fellows they were, too. To snatch a treasured feathery or gutty from the Old Course, one of them would hide under the bridge of the Swilcan Burn, waiting in complete silence until a golfer hit his ball into the water. He would then perform a quick and furtive stirring of the stream, discolouring it so that the golfer would not be able to see and recover his ball. When the stream had cleared (and the golfer gone angrily on his way), there would be another ball to add to the lads' collection.

While these young Scottish enthusiasts were improvising golf at St Andrews, a seven-year-old lad by the name of Harry Vardon was learning the game in Jersey in the Channel Isles. He and his friends were of similar age to the St Andreans and were suffering much the same problems. They had no links, no clubs, no balls, no money.

'We surmounted all these difficulties,' said Vardon, 'for we laid out a special course of our very own. It consisted of only four holes, each of them about fifty yards long, but – for boys of seven – quite long enough. We made our teeing-grounds, smoothed out the greens and were soon ready for play.'

In the absence of gutties, they played with big white marbles, called 'taws', about half the size of an ordinary golf ball. For clubs, they cut heads from oak trees and shafts from white or black thorn. They bored holes with red-hot pokers and tightened the shafts with wedges. When the oak heads chipped and cracked, they soled them with tin. Ambitious undertakings, weren't they, for young lads of only seven? But in this respect and many others there's a remarkable similarity between the boy golfers of St Andrews and those of Jersey. Both were determined to play golf, despite all the difficulties and shortages, and managed to do so without outside help.

Golf-writer extraordinary Bernard Darwin began as a boy, at Felixstowe, where his family used to spend summer holidays. He was a solitary player because there were no other boys to play with but, as the family sometimes stayed in the clubhouse, his opportunities for golf were excellent. Even so, because he was so young and no one offered to play with him, he became what he termed 'a young outlaw leading a lawless, reckless life, squeezing my way in and out between the grown-up couples and playing one particular hole, the second, over and over again. I daresay fifty times a day. It was a short hole and with a wild rush I could play it while the grown-ups were holing out on the first green; then wriggling back to the tee, keeping under the lee of the Martello tower and so hope to dodge my way in again.'

Bernard's idol was Willie Fernie, the Felixstowe professional,

Open champion of 1883, who once came within inches of destroying him with a hooked shot and half-topped ball that rattled against the black sleepers of the bunker in which he cowered. How fortunate we are that Darwin was spared from Fernie's venomous hook. The literature of golf is so enriched by him.

Years later, in America, the supreme amateur champion Bobby Jones began playing just after his fifth birthday; and another great American amateur, Francis Ouimet, started at seven. Both began on makeshift courses with makeshift clubs. Bobby and the neighbourhood kids made their own course of two holes, of the same length. One was in the roadway in front of Bobby's house, and the other ran into a deep ditch alongside the main road.

'Sometimes when the fairway or road was hard we could hit a ball that would go rolling into the ditch from what constituted the tee,' said Bobby. And although he never made a hole in one on an actual course until he was twenty-five, he made a hole in one into the ditch several times before he was six years old!

Francis Ouimet, living near the Country Club in Brookline, spent his seven-year-old days – particularly on the way to and from school – looking for gutties in the rough. In this way, he acquired more balls than he could use. But, sadly, he had no club. He used to borrow his brother's only club and practise swinging in the back yard, which wasn't very exciting. But then his brother discovered that Francis could exchange three dozen old balls for a new mashie in a Boston store. Thus equipped, the Ouimet brothers marked out a three-hole course in a cow pasture near their home and, once more against the odds, a champion was on the way. At nineteen years of age (with a ten-year-old caddie!) Francis Ouimet won the United States Open from the illustrious Vardon and Ray.

Today, the golfing cradle rocks in other parts of the world. In Spain and Japan, there's a similar awakening of boy golfers, and schoolboy caddies are swinging treasured clubs on the boundaries of the courses. Everlastingly pitching balls about, chipping off bare ground, putting out, over and over again. Like the youngsters of St Andrews, Jersey, Felixstowe and East Lake, Atlanta, they scratch a game wherever they can. On improvised patches of ground, regardless of tight lies, they chip the ball back and forth and hole imaginary putts for Open titles.

Who then doubts that from these simple beginnings came Seve Ballesteros's beautiful short game? At seven, Seve was given his first club, or – to be more precise – part of a club, a rusty old 3-iron head. For shafts, Seve gathered sticks and cut them to length, whittled them to shape for the hosel, soaked them overnight in a bucket of water to achieve a tight fit. And (shades of Vardon and his friends!) the balls he used were small round pebbles from the beach. Ammunition to fire a boy's enthusiastic dreams and allow him to make a determined attack on the game, he lost no time in filling his pockets with them.

I doubt whether Seve knew then that the great Vardon, six times winner of the Open, had improvised in much the same way – or that his ingenuity would lead him to capture that same coveted title and trophy, thousands of pebbles away ...

36 Meditation upon a Broomstick

In the game of golf (as at the Harvest Festival where an unknown mouse eats through a sheaf of oats), things are not always what they seem. For example, in the hands of the late Ernest Jones, a handkerchief was not simply a handkerchief and a pocketknife not simply a pocketknife. Separately, they may have been used for wiping Ernest's nose and cutting a piece of string, but together they synchronized his theory of swinging a golf club. As many readers will know, Jones attached a pocketknife to the corner of a handkerchief and, swinging both weighted handkerchief and a golf club together, cleverly demonstrated 'true swinging movement' as distinct from 'unwanted leverage'.

W.S. Gilbert's catchy couplet in *HMS Pinafore*:

Things are seldom what they seem,
skim milk masquerades as cream

brings to mind Henry Cotton's motor-car tyre masquerading as a golfing teaching aid, particularly when it's old and soft and receptive to a good hiding with a golf club. For the last quarter-century, the Maestro's used the idea successfully in coaching and golf-clinic demonstrations, and his tireless advocacy of the tyre-drill has strengthened the hands, wrists and resolution of golfers all over the world.

'What's all this got to do with a broomstick?' asks the chap in the cloth cap and muddy shoes, and I think it's time I explained that I take my title from Swift, for more than one reason.

Some 300 years ago, Jonathan Swift (best known for *Gulliver's Travels*) observed a broomstick lying in the corner of a room and, in a flight of fancy, wrote an essay in which he imagined it flourishing in the forest, the stick full of sap and its branches full of leaves. 'But now,' he said sadly, 'at best, it is the reverse of what it was, a tree turned upside down, the branches on the earth and the root in the air.' A tree masquerading as a broom, or a broom masquerading as a tree.

Ah, but I ask you, what would Swift have made of a broom masquerading as a golf club?

In America today, golfers eager to cure a slice are being advised to swing a broom. It's one of the more unusual tuitional ideas and has been thought up by Hank Johnson, head professional at the North River Golf and Yacht Club, Tuscaloosa. Apparently, his young daughter, a high-school cheerleader, asked him to help with her swing and, like Swift before him, observing a broom lying in a corner of the outside patio, he imagined it as a golf club, rather than a broom, and demonstrated his theories with it in one easy drill.

'I was amazed how quickly she was relating to the feel I was trying to convey,' said Hank, 'and the construction of the broom had a lot to do with it. I began incorporating a broom in my teaching at the club, and it certainly helped. Now I never teach without one.'

To distinguish between open and closed clubface, which I gather is vital to the outcome, you paint one side of the bristles red and the other green. Also, you add a bit of tape at 43 inches on the broomstick (the standard length of a driver), and, these few modifications done, simply sweep the broom through the impact area, rotating hands and forearms and turning the colours of the brush from red to green. Hank assures golfers that a few minutes' practising each day will turn a weak slice into a controlled draw.

Well, now. Who's going to be the brave guinea-pig and first to paint the kitchen broom red and green? I dare say that Hank's experiments were quietly condoned in the interests of golf professionalism, and I don't suppose he had to suffer the cross-examination you and I would be subjected to if the domestic arrangements of the home were put in disorder because of a missing kitchen broom.

A voice of shrill vociferation would be heard from kitchen-depths.

'For the third time of asking, what has happened to the kitchen broom? It can't just get up and walk away of its own accord. Where is it?'

'It's in Dad's golf bag.'

An exclamation of undisguised astonishment is heard, together with a rather impatient and grim reply.

'You can't have heard what I said. I wasn't asking about a golf bag. I was asking for the kitchen broom!'

'I *know*. I *heard* you. It's in his golf bag. The bristles have been painted red and green, and there's some yellow tape on the handle.'

Fortunately for us, these are only imaginary thoughts of what might happen if we were unwise enough to take Hank's advice. Much as we applaud the idea and do not doubt its effectiveness, we simply dare not risk the painful scenes that would ensue. Our *slight* slice seems the lesser of two evils.

Finding new hiding-places for Henry Cotton's old tyre is a big enough problem as it is. The blessed thing is always being discovered and dragged out for the refuse collectors to take away. And it's only by those admirable gentlemen understanding our golfing foibles – and secretly handing it back – that we manage to keep on strengthening and improving our hand action, as Henry says we should.

37   The Henpecked Fraternity

The subject of henpecked golfers was expounded recently in yet another of the Old Codger's boring monologues in the clubhouse bar. Holding his gin-and-tonic in a strong, Judy Rankin, four-knuckle grip, he prefaced his remarks on the henpecked fraternity by explaining why Seve Ballesteros is the world's greatest golfer.

'It's because he's still a *bachelor*. Still a single, unmarried chap, without a fear in the world. A golfer ready to open up his shoulders, toss care to the winds and go hell-for-leather for every shot in the book without being apprehensive of a wife's criticism at the end of the round.'

Needless to say, as is usual when the Old Codger is holding forth, these remarks were largely ignored by a mostly married and worn-out audience. It was as though a number of flagging, somnolent cats were refusing to be drawn by a plastic mouse pirouetting in front of their whiskers. Equally, the younger men and bachelors in the bar said nothing, their talk of the day's birdies and steady consumption of bitter beer keeping them occupied. However, faint acknowledgement came nervously from a couple of once-a-week, nine-hole Category 4s, in a murmur of mutual understanding.

'I tell you, gentlemen, there's scarcely an instance in the amateur or professional game in which a golfer's form has been known to improve after marriage,' continued the Old Codger. 'But, by jingo, there's bags of evidence to the contrary to prove that a golfer's game goes to pot once he sets foot outside the church. As he walks with that silly grin on his face under an archway of once-used 1-irons, his game begins to fall apart. From then on, he slips from category to category in the amateur ranks; and, if he's a professional, his pay-cheques get smaller and smaller. Gone are the days of Porches and Volvos for holing in one. Henceforward, he's kept busy with extraneous matters, like learning not to pick up the baby by the ankle – and not to toss it down in odd corners as if it were a golf bag.'

At this point in the monologue the Old Codger introduced a little mimicry and character acting.

'*Look at how he's holding the baby! Like she was a golf bag! Put her down. You're not supposed to swing her like a pitching wedge! You'll make her sick!*'

'I once knew a fellow, the keenest of golfers. We used to play seven days a week on all the best courses. His handicap was down to 2, and scratch for him would have been an absolute certainty – but what did he do? Met a girl from Sunningdale, fell hopelessly in love and got married.

'Need I say more? He never set foot inside the clubhouse inside the next six months, and when at last he did, it was always a case of "Not able to stay long" and "Sorry, old chap, got to go now." Poor chap took on a sort of *hunted* look, as though a hand was about to tap him on the shoulder and remind him of the washing-up.

'The golfing transformation was unbelievable. It makes me shudder to think of it. The few times we played together after his marriage he scarcely hit a decent shot. The power had gone. His handicap was a good ten strokes worse than before – about 12, I'd say – and one never quite knew where one was with him. Often, he couldn't manage to play more than nine holes. He wanted to rush off suddenly, remembering he'd promised to get his wife a pound of tomatoes or a tin of custard powder, or maybe collect a skirt from the cleaners. On one occasion, after we'd played only seven holes, he had to dash off urgently and choose some new curtains.

'I heard later he'd sold his clubs and bought himself a poodle. He thought it would keep his wife's poodle company, and his chief interest seemed to be in shampooing them, though I believe he still managed a game of croquet occasionally.

'What's that? Tell you the story of the henpecked golfing society? Of course I will. Henpecked golfers are no more of a rarity than henpecked all-in-wrestlers or night-club bouncers. And what about egg-farmers? Could anyone be more henpecked? I mean, they're for *real*, aren't they?'

'This was a group of henpecked golfers, about a dozen strong. They planned to form themselves into a secret society to stop their wives grousing about their frequency of play. At their first meeting in the clubhouse in a private room, as they sat talking and planning things, the dozen wives – who'd been tipped off about the meeting – suddenly burst into the room. Well, of course, there was such a panic and stampede! Eleven of the husbands promptly skedaddled through a side door, leaving one slow-witted chap remaining to give the explanation.

'The wives laughed contemptuously at the success of their raid and went off in high spirits to celebrate. The eleven golfers then agreed unanimously that the brave twelfth man who had not run away should be appointed their president. But, on returning to offer him the post, they found that he'd died of fright.'

38   By the Light of the Moon

'And hand in hand, on the edge of the sand, they danced by the light of the moon.'

Making an oblique approach – rather like hitting one off the socket – readers will see that I take my title from Edward Lear's 'The Owl and the Pussy-cat', and some may ask what an owl and a pussy-cat have to do with the game of golf. Even more imaginative ones may jump to the conclusion that 'the edge of the sand' is about to lead to a tedious dissertation on the best way to escape from the fringes or lips of bunkers, but the truth is much more simple. I'm about to offer a few observations on playing golf by the light of the moon.

An improbable subject? Well, there's little moonlighting on the links these days, I think. But quite a lot took place in years gone by and, though you may not be aware of it, golf's greatest champions played and practised in the moonlight.

Whilst still very young and full of boyish enthusiasm, Harry Vardon played golf in the moonlight with his friends in the Channel Islands. He said: 'We practised our very elementary kind of golf whenever we could, and were soon enthusiastic. I remember particularly that many of our best matches were played in the moonlight. The moon seemed to shine more clearly at Jersey than in England, and we could see splendidly.'

He and three other boys would go out together on a moonlight night to play, usually with a few marbles at stake. To prevent lost balls, one boy would go on ahead to watch and listen for the faint thud of their fall, while the other three drove from the tee.

'I am sorry to say that our keenness in those days led us to disregard certain principles of the sportsman's code of honour which we appreciated better as we grew up,' said Harry. 'What I mean is that the watcher was often handicapped in a way that he little suspected, for when he went back to the tee, and we went forward and found that our balls were not always so well up as we had hoped, we gave them a gentle kick forwards; for in the dim light we were able to do this unknown to each other.'

Another great golfer, Bobby Jones, was a young moonlighter too. He said: 'I remember back in my high school days, I was living within the range of a good iron shot from the East Lake course, and on nights when the moon was out, I used to go over to the club and putt, with a friend and neighbour, on the practice green near the tenth tee. The moonlight, of course, revealed the hole, and it also made visible the more prominent slopes and undulations, but it kindly left obscured the more subtle slopes and irregularities – wormcasts and the like. In this half-revealing light, it was a source of wonderment to my friend and me that we invariably putted better than in broad daylight, especially when it came to holing out from distances up to eight or ten feet.'

Bobby thought there must be something to be learned from moonlight putting, and thought it might be the fact that golfers who putted well on good and bad greens had schooled themselves to see a putting green as he and his friends used to see it in the moonlight.

We turn now to the present-day and to a great – some say the greatest – modern golfer, Seve Ballesteros. There's a remarkable similarity between Bobby Jones's experience of putting in the moonlight and Seve's remarks about night-putting. For Seve says: 'Practising your putting when it's almost dark helps your golf putting habits and gives you confidence. It does this for one reason – you can't see anything (except maybe a dim hole in the distance), and this takes away the temptation to watch where the ball is going after you hit it. Instead, you can keep your head down and watch only the line of your stroke – which is the way you should putt.'

More than fifty years separate these two great golfers' experiences, yet each advocates putting practice in the semi-dark. Remarkable!

Of course we have heard of Seve roaming the golf links by the light of the moon, sharpening up his approach shots to the green. As a boy in Pedrena, he used to sneak onto the course and play in the dark or moonlight, much as Vardon and Jones before him. To paraphrase Sir Walter Scott, 'If thou wouldst view the golf greens aright, Go visit them by the pale moonlight.'

Golfers have achieved most things on the links in the

moonlight. They've accepted wagers to go round in a specified number of strokes – and done so. They've played a complete eighteen holes without losing a single ball. And even the much-acclaimed feat of holing in one has been accomplished by the light of the moon.

Meanwhile, if you're feeling dissatisfied with orthodox golf (or perhaps somewhat exhausted at the sheer pace of stamp-collecting), try your luck and see how many ten-footers you can sink by the light of the moon. But *watch out*, for while you're quietly concentrating on your putting – keeping your head down and watching only the line of stroke, as Seve says you should – a transparent, emaciated figure may wander silently over the turf. You see, it's long been rumoured that every moonlight night throughout the year a ghost goes round a golf course which, for obvious reasons, must remain secret.

What's that you say? *In how many?*

39 As They Lie on the Couch

This is a somewhat poignant story of a golfer who became so disturbed by the game that he reached the sad state of believing himself to be a golf-trolley. Indeed, so desperate did he become with 'golf trolley anxiety' that he was compelled to stop playing for a while and lie day after day on a psychiatrist's couch.

His wife was the first to notice his fantasies. She observed him walking round and round the lawn, holding his arm above his head in the shape of a swan's neck, and continually stopping and waiting patiently before moving on again. Hidden behind the summerhouse, she watched him zigzagging about the lawn and, as he passed by for the seventh time, she suddenly shot from cover and said: 'What d'you think you're doing, Fred?'

'Doing?' he replied. 'It's simple enough. Can't you see I'm a golf-trolley?'

Rather a shock for her of course. But golfing wives – like absent-minded electricians – are used to shocks and know how to cope. She wasn't an excitable type given to kicking about, cracking her knuckles or going off into hysterics. She simply said: 'I see, Fred, love. And I take it that your arm is held high above your head because it's the trolley's handle?'

Fred looked up at his crooked arm and smiled. 'So you guessed.'

A sound, sensible girl, well used to absorbing the idiosyncratic fantasies of golfers, she didn't tell him he was being downright ridiculous. Nor did she lecture him or say she was afraid he'd reached the stage of being unable to separate the gravy from the prunes. Instead, she packed him off to the doctor (temporarily retracting his arm and stowing it away at his side), who in turn lost no time in re-packing him off to a psychiatrist.

Well, there's Fred on his way to the couch; and you may well declare the story fantastic and not unlike someone conceding you a nine-inch putt. But I doubt whether it will raise many golfing eyebrows. Old dogs and even older golfers tend to be somewhat stingy with their emotions. They have to be, or their bones and balls will be snatched away from under their noses.

Realizing how unbearable it would be for the reader to miss anything at this point in the story, I took the trouble to obtain a transcript of the tape made at this chap's first session with his psychiatrist and offer it as evidence of what can be done to help off-the-beam golfers suffering from extraordinary fantasies. Incidentally, not least of the transcript's interest lies in the fact that – as you'll see – the psychiatrist is an experienced golfer.

PSYCHIATRIST: Come in, old chap. No need to signal and wave your hand like that. I may wear dark glasses, but I can see you perfectly well.

FRED: I wasn't waving. As my doctor told you, I'm a golf-trolley and that's my handle sticking up ready to move off for a round.

PSYCHIATRIST: A golf-trolley, hey? Well, fold yourself in half and roll onto that couch – and let me tell you about my week-end birdie with a 4-iron at the 5th. I decided to hit it with a bit of draw for a change and …

FRED: Is it common?

PSYCHIATRIST: A birdie at the 5th with a 4-iron? You know it isn't common.

FRED: No. I mean golf-trolley anxiety, the thing I'm suffering from. Do many golfers get it?

PSYCHIATRIST: A few, old chap. Mostly Category 4 players. But by far more common are the fellows who think they're ball-washers of the vertical, brush-up-and-down type. They're usually Category 2 and 3. But all players get twitchy. Category 1 is stuffed to the brim with blokes who believe they're motor-car tyres. You know, the Cotton-hit-the-tyre-theory.

FRED: Is it for men only?

PSYCHIATRIST: Is what for men only?

FRED: Being a golf-trolley. Are there any *lady* golf-trolleys?

PSYCHIATRIST: I suppose so. One or two, I guess.

FRED: How can you tell the difference?

PSYCHIATRIST: Search me. You're the trolley. *You* should know. Anyway, lady golfers are usually something much more simple and attractive. For instance, one came to me recently following a stiff slimming course and told me she was a flagstick.

FRED: What about rakes?

PSYCHIATRIST: Rakes?

FRED: Bunker-rakes and bunker-rake anxieties.

PSYCHIATRIST: Can't say I've treated them. But let's get back to golf-trolleys, Fred. Have you done much popping in and out of car-boots?

FRED: (rather hesitantly): Er – no.

PSYCHIATRIST: Well, then. Have you done much standing about or hanging on the wall in corners of draughty garages and sheds right through the night?

FRED (even more hesitantly): Er – no.

PSYCHIATRIST: Are you narrow or wide?

FRED: Narrow or wide?

PSYCHIATRIST: Wheels.

FRED (blushing and confused and taking a wild guess): Narrow.

PSYCHIATRIST: Then I shouldn't worry if I were you, Fred. Most clubs won't allow you on the course. You're a dead loss, especially in soft going. I think you'll find your anxiety will shove off quite suddenly and you'll start playing again pretty soon. It might be an idea to begin without a ball at first, like Henry Cotton's visitor at Sotogrande. He went out with a full set of clubs and a caddie and played a complete round without a ball. All make-believe. Try it, Fred. It's much more fun than being a golf-trolley. You can hit long drives, splash out of bunkers and water hazards and go right the way round without losing a single ball. You just use an invisible one.

FRED: Oh, good. I might move up into Category 3 in that way. It's a super idea for medal play.

PSYCHIATRIST: You must excuse me now, Fred. I've got an undertaker coming in who's having to manage with a skeleton staff, and there's a lady golfer who thinks she's a tee towel.

Looking back at what I've written, I think I ought to say that Fred's name isn't Fred. I just thought up the name in order to preserve his anonymity and avoid embarrassment. His real name is Wilfred ...

40   The Links of Tilling

The game of golf appears frequently in the light-hearted novels of E.F. Benson (principally in *Miss Mapp*), and the incidents on the links are not unlike those in the Wodehouse golf stories. Both authors were writing of around the twenties period and of eccentric golfers performing inexpertly and becoming irritated, petulant and beastly to one another. But Benson's golfers of Tilling make light of old arguments and go from their homes to catch the 11.20 steam-tram to the golf course each morning.

Incidentally, Benson lived for many years in Henry James's house – Lamb House – at Rye, and it's a pretty safe bet that the fictional links of Tilling were really those of Rye.

The two golfers we read of most in Benson's delightful descriptions are Major Flint (a big, soldier-like man who, after spending many years in India, is still given to sudden commands in Hindustani) and Captain Puffin (lame, short and quite unimpressive) who play golf together in the mornings and then rest up in the afternoons. 'As a rule, they played golf together in the morning, reposed in the afternoon, as could easily be verified by anyone standing on a still day in the road between their houses and listening to the loud and rhythmical breathings that fanned the tranquil air.'

Even so, these retired gentlemen sometimes tackle thirty-six holes in a single day without a qualm. Their addiction to golf is such that they have no hesitation in leaving church during the sermon to catch the 12.20 tram out to the links.

Retired officers of HM Services, their match-play golf takes the form of tense battles between Army and Navy. Halving holes in sixes and sevens (and possibly twenty-sevens for all we know), they go at one another passionately with nervous drives skyed to prodigious heights that finish in nasty lies in boarded bunkers. When not victorious, their excuses are as predictable as ever. The Major invariably blames a doubtful wound which

might be anything from a vaccination mark to a sabre-cut, while
the Captain always goes dead lame when beaten.

In this respect, one can't help thinking of the golfer who
asked his opponent on the tee: 'Is there anything wrong with
you?' Indignant, the opponent replied: 'No. Why?' 'Well, I
thought I'd just ask, for I don't seem to have beaten a fit golfer
for many a month!'

In one match, Puffin claims a hole from Flint under the rules
of golf, and a terrible row occurs. The two hobble into the
clubhouse separately, no longer on speaking terms. But
Benson's unflagging imagination soon brings them back on

friendly terms for our continued amusement. The angry Major, loudly demanding whisky, is told that he can't be served till six o'clock. And it is at this point that the Captain produces a large flask of whisky from his locker and proceeds to mix himself a long, strong drink. Finding it quite impossible to be proud and proper any longer, the Major twirls his moustache, clears his throat and speaks.

'Upon my word, Puffin, I'm ashamed of myself for not taking my defeat better. A man's no business to let a game ruffle him.'

'Oh, that's all right, Major,' says Puffin. 'I know it's awfully hard to lose like a gentleman.'

He lets this sink in, then adds: 'Have a drink, old chap?'

In another tense Army-Navy set-to, played in awesome weather, a drenching storm causes conflicting opinions. Puffin, being three up, refuses Flint's request to call off the match. But Flint, remembering that Puffin's game usually goes to pieces when it rains, elects to play on, and the match becomes notable for its many disagreeable incidents. The Major's driver, slippery from rain, flies from his grasp and lands in a pool of water. His ball lands in another pool. A hole or so later, the Captain falls flat on his face while attempting to lash his fifth shot home to the green. Each player stymies the other and then holes the wrong ball by mistake. Another argument breaks out over the correct procedure when a ball lies in a rabbit-scrape or on tram-lines. The Major loses a new ball and, most comical and inventive of all, a mushroom is found on one of the greens between the Captain's ball and the hole.

That evening, while recovering from the drenching on the links at the Major's home, the pair overdo things with the whisky bottle and begin to boast of putting sporting challenges in *The Times*:

'Retired Major challenges any gentleman of forty-five years or over to a shooting match in the morning, followed by half a dozen rounds with four-ounce gloves, a game of golf, eighteen holes, in the afternoon, and a billiards match of two hundred up after tea.'

Captain Puffin, not to be outdone, drafts a similar advertisement:

'Retired Captain, aged fifty, who'll take on all comers of forty-two or over, at a steeple-chase, round of golf, billiards match, hopping match, gymnastic competition, swinging Indian clubs.'

As the night and the whisky-drinking go on, an argument

develops over Puffin's inability to drink a large measure of whisky and clearly enunciate the word 'hippopotamus' afterwards. At this stage, things get so out of hand that they culminate in the Major's challenging the Captain to a duel with pistols on the golf links the following morning, seconds to be notified and so on. Not surprisingly, in the sober light of morning, both Major and Captain are horror-stricken at the thought of a pistol fight. So much so, that each decides to leave Tilling at once by train. But in an anti-climax they meet providentially at the railway station, immediately make their peace – and decide to play golf together instead!

These Benson golf scenes are great fun, and those I've mentioned are supplemented by others. Miss Mapp practising mashie shots from her lawn, in which she makes dreadful holes, bounces the ball off a garden wall to bring it back to her feet. But even Miss Mapp learns to hit shots over her snowdrops without beheading them.

Benson also introduces us to Tipsipoozie, a lean Irish terrier, inconsiderately tethered to a bag of golf clubs. Poor Tipsipoozie decides to pursue one of the characters down a station platform, still towing the clubs after him, and becomes so entangled that he can only fall down, snapping at the clubs, the station-master and all the porters.

41   Like a Caddie Swings

The late James Agate, *Daily Express* columnist and dramatic critic of the *Sunday Times* for over twenty years before his death in 1947, left many interesting notes on the game of golf, which he loved dearly and played enthusiastically as he travelled the country on his playgoing and other journalistic affairs. An amateur golfer of more than average ability (nine holes in 39 at Royal Lytham and St Anne's), Agate declared himself unable to stick amateurism in any form.

'I would rather give up the game altogether than play with amateurs of no style,' he said. 'Half my fun in golf has been the intense pleasure I have got out of watching the professional stuff. I loathe amateur acting and any golf swing in which I cannot detect the caddie.'

One of Agate's friends rather comically subscribed to this viewpoint by stating that Cleopatra made a mess of her love-making the day she turned amateur!

Agate once said that, if he were asked to name off-hand the six best prose writers of all time – and also pressed to give the reason for his choice, he would say it was because they never thought about style and so achieved 'a rhythm like that of the golf caddie who does not know how to swing a club, but just swings it'. We will never know what his chosen six (Job, Shakespeare, Bunyan, Defoe, Dickens and Shaw) would have made of his somewhat eccentric analogy, for only Dickens and Shaw lived in golfing times, and even they might have required further enlightenment on the all-important caddie-swings.

With the week's playgoing completed, Agate would turn his thoughts to golf and motor perhaps thirty or forty miles to seek out a match with a professional or his assistant – and ideally to Agate's liking one which ended on the last green. If his playgoing commitments were at the seaside, so much the better, for the natural links were there ready and waiting, and a professional opponent would once again be engaged. For example, his notes tell us of a ding-dong match at Brighton against a young professional who gave him four bisques. At the 17th, Agate became dormy one. 'This unnerved the boy, who hit a poor drive, while I got mine away superbly.' But Agate's opponent then put his brassie within six yards of the pin. 'This unnerved me, and I cut my mashie slightly so that the ball, pitching on the green, ran all around the right-hand bunker before toppling in. I got out too well and so the match was halved. An exciting game, a good, modest young pro and a lovely day.'

On another occasion, at Thorpe Bay, he played with a new assistant. 'Enormous hands, feet big enough for two policemen, leggy like a colt, he drives some 300 yards and should make a golfer some day.' But Agate described the assistant's swing as too loose and 'needing a bit of stomach to play his shots against'. He said the young pro's swing was so free and full that he was inclined, when he let out completely, 'to swing round and face the wicket-keeper'.

A higher standard of golf occurred in 1932, when Agate challenged R.A. Whitcombe (Open Champion, 1938) to play the best ball of himself and a young pro on the understanding that Whitcombe would concede six bisques. The course was Parkstone, where Whitcombe was the professional, and Agate knew he would have a match on his hands, for Whitcombe had once holed the Bournemouth course in 61.

Agate began in fine style with 4,4,3,5,4,5 and matched Whitcombe's figures without help from his young partner. Six holes played, the match was all square, with all bisques intact. But then Whitcombe played so well that, with three holes left to play, the Agate team was only one up with one bisque in hand. Later, on the seventeenth tee, they were one up with all bisques gone. But the drama was not yet played out, for the young pro pitched stone-dead for a half at the 17th, and then knocked in a twenty-yard putt for a 3 at the 18th. Whitcombe, on the green only ten yards from the stick, just missed for his birdie 2, and the Agate partnership won a first-class struggle.

'Whitcombe, who is like some genial, witty bear, played magnificently,' wrote Agate, little knowing that six years later the West-countryman would prove himself a master of the game in a tearing gale at Royal St George's, Sandwich, to take the Open title.

After playing a round on a strange course, Agate once asked the golfers in the bar how one was expected to play the fifteenth hole of some 210 yards. 'It's too far for an iron and too strictly guarded for a wood,' said Agate.

To this enquiry, a pompous ass (Agate's description) boomed: 'My daughter is invariably over the green with a 2-iron.'

To which an insignificant little man in the corner of the bar said quietly: 'Then why doesn't she take a No.3?'

Agate told a story of a well-known heavyweight boxer, who was also a keen golfer. Approaching the green he saw a young urchin climb over a fence and steal his ball. Over the same fence went the boxer, to find himself outside a cottage, with a huge navvy standing in the doorway.

'Your kid has pinched my ball,' said the boxer.

'If yer want yer —— ball yer must —— —— come and get it!' replied the navvy.

'OK,' said the boxer, shooting out a straight left. And, stepping over the body, he went upstairs, dragged the kid from under the bed, spanked him, recovered his ball, returned to the green, replaced it and placidly remarked: 'Let me see, partner. I think I'm playing the like.'

One of Agate's most amusing little notes of 1935 read: 'To-night on the golf links at Clacton and against the setting sun, I saw an aeroplane with the streamer ''Eat Sharp's Mickey Mouse Toffee!'' '

42   *Unwittingly Fading*

As a special treat, in the clubhouse bar, the Old Codger gives us his all-too-familiar golfing monologue. With a gin-and-tonic held in an interlocking grip, he tells us of the changes now taking place.

'All today's courses are built on hillsides that get steeper every time you play them. Every elevated tee and green is more elevated than it was in my young days, with far fewer handrails to assist golfers up many more steps. Also, no matter where I choose to play, it's a devil of a sight longer walk from the clubhouse to the first tee and between all the greens and the next teeing-ground.

'The distance up our fifth fairway is twice what it used to be. I know that for certain because it takes me twice as many shots and more than twice the time to reach the green. And it's all on account of that damned steep hill just short of the green. It was never there in my young days. It's like climbing the side of the clubhouse.

'It's one of life's mysteries how they made the alteration. I never saw bulldozers working on it or even heard of its authorization. And when I asked the Greens Committee for an explanation, the members just laughed and looked at me strangely, as if I was some kind of nut. I guess they were embarrassed at my criticism, possibly because I seem to be one of the few (perhaps the only one?) who has noticed it.

'But they're a damned devious lot. Busy as a bag of ferrets, yet swearing they haven't had a bulldozer anywhere near the course. But as I said: "How can you raise a bloody great lump like that with no more than a bucket and spade?"

'And, if you tackle the Secretary, he just looks at you steel-eyed, as though you were guilty of not replacing a whopping big divot. But as Stevenson remarked, the cruellest lies are often told in silence, aren't they?

'Why don't they stop mucking about with courses? They're even making the *holes* lower than they were. Reaching down to pick out the ball is much farther than it used to be. And have you noticed the holes inside the cups for the flagsticks to plug into are being made *smaller*? If you haven't, then no doubt you've noticed how much longer it takes, and what an annoying fiddle it is, to put the flagstick back.

'And while I'm on about flagsticks, do tell me if you can *see* the blessed things. Damned if I can. What have golf clubs done to make them so *distant* and *invisible*? They used to stand out like Cleopatra's Needle.

'Another thing. Have you noticed how difficult it is to read the writing on the ball? Makers' names and numbers get smaller and smaller until they're quite indecipherable. Is there some conspiracy afoot to make golfers go *blind*? It's absurd to say that a person of my age needs glasses on the links, but the only way I can identify my ball is to back off and hold the confounded thing out at arm's length.

'The small print on scorecards is monstrous. Only the other day, I stepped back into a water hazard trying to decipher the number and length of the hole – and, after all that, I failed. Practically the only way I can learn the yardage and stroke numbers – not to mention local rules – is to get someone to read them out to me, and that's not the best of arrangements because, for some odd reason, today's golfers speak in such low and indistinct voices that I've the utmost difficulty in hearing them.

'Look at the small print that's being used on clubhouse and locker-room noticeboards. Why, even restaurant menus get farther and farther away as I hold them out in front of me, so that I squint and become cross-eyed. Indeed, I push back my chair so *far*, I'm almost sitting with the golfers at the next table.

'All golf equipment is being made more difficult. Clubs are a *dead* weight. One of our older members fell on his knees in a bunker simply because his sand-iron was too heavy. It literally *threw* him off his feet. Such a pity, too, for it was a present from his young wife to mark his eighty-ninth birthday – and he's pretty sure she didn't choose it deliberately. But, that's another thing about golf, you never know with young wives, do you? She's been playing a lot with the professional.

'What does it take to make a golfer think of giving up the game? Well, the answer doesn't take much looking for. It comes right at the start of the round, when you're faced with the simple act of putting on your spiked shoes. Or, at any rate, what used to be a *simple* act.

'Why have shoe-designers turned nasty all of a sudden and made their eyelets so small you can hardly *see* them? And why are laces thicker and more easily knotted? It makes golfers stamp and cuss, where they used to smile and hum.

'But some golfers declare that even *noses* are changing. One old lad I know complains bitterly of a dewdrop constantly interfering with his swing-pattern. Only the other day, it caused him to top his tee-shot to the long seventeenth and send it but a few feeble yards along the ground.

' "You know what happened there, don't you?" he asked.

' "No. What?"

' "I was put off again by that damned dewdrop. It was wavering about on my backswing and decided to drop off just as I started down from the top. How the devil can a chap hope to play a decent game with a nose like mine?"

'Well, there was no answer to that, was there? But, you know, even excuses aren't what they were in my younger days. I remember phoning an old friend of eighty-five and inviting him to an early morning greensome.

' "Sorry, old fellow, I'm afraid I can't," he croaked. "I'm in bed with a nurse."

'Sometime after luncheon, you could have knocked me down with a tee-peg when I spotted the old devil playing nine holes with her!'

43 Only the Dead Know Stymies

'Dere's no guy livin' dat knows de stymie t'roo an' t'roo, because it'd take a guy a lifetime to find his way aroun' duh goddam ting.'

Readers familiar with Thomas Wolfe's short story 'Only The Dead Know Brooklyn' will recognize my paraphrasing immediately. Written wholly in the Brooklyn idiom, insofar as the stymie's history is concerned, it serves our purpose very well. For it would indeed take a guy more than a lifetime to know the stymie through and through, quite apart from finding his way around the goddam thing, which in most cases was virtually impossible. Even if there was a borrow on the green to help you, there was always the risk of knocking your adversary's ball into the hole and so damaging your prospect of victory. The stymie has been abolished from the game for so long now (over thirty years) that only senior golfers have memories of the exciting effect it had to on match-play golf. And finally, on 1 April 1984, golf's last link with the stymie was broken. A change of rule from that date now permits a player to lift and mark his ball if its closeness to the hole assists his opponent, thus ending an ancient custom dating back to 1744, first introduced by the Honourable Company of Edinburgh Golfers, who then played on the links of Leith but subsequently moved in 1891 to Muirfield, the now-famous Open Championship links.

That the stymie had to die in 1984 doubtless came easily to it. It was often what was known as *dead*, so that one ball completely barred the other ball's entry to the hole. Also, it was always nearing death, for abolition was frequently proposed and gravely considered. Retrospectively, the rule changed in 1937, so that a ball lying six inches from the hole had to be lifted, but –

no less than 148 years before, in 1789 – the first six-inch rule was introduced, permitting the lifting of a ball if the balls were within six inches of one another. The reason for this seems comical today, for it was to prevent players from deliberately aiming a putt at an opponent's ball, not only to clear the stymie but also to knock it into a worse position – and in severe cases into a bunker! *'Take that, you cur!'*

Before the making of the 1937 rule, a questionnaire was sent to sixty-four qualifiers in the American Amateur Championship, as follows:

A   (1) Do you like or dislike the stymie?
      (2) Why?
B   (1) Do you think the stymie should remain in the game or not?
      (2) Why?
C   (1) What would you recommend as an alternative to the stymie?
      (2) Have you ever observed in practice the alternative you recommend?

Many varied replies were received. Some golfers gave vital reasons for retention of the stymie and strong opinions were put of their liking and disliking. But the questions asked in C merely added to the stymie's complexities. However, the stymie was still so highly regarded that the majority of the amateurs were in favour of keeping it in the game. For example, one famous ex-amateur and Open American champion said: 'I like the stymie. Match-play is dull without it. The stymie should remain in the game. It has successfully stood the test of time.' Another former champion answered: 'I like the stymie. I cannot conceive of an alternative to take its place. Golf is a game of art and skill. To negotiate a stymie is a skilful shot.' Perhaps, like the great amateur John L. Low, long before them, who said: 'We had better keep our old foe, the stymie, for if we kill him we shall rob ourselves of many a nice-looking excuse,' they felt no match had ever been lost entirely by the stymie rule.

Today's golfer may ask just what negotiating stymies involved and exactly what skills were asked for. Well, advice in plenty was given by the day's leading amateurs and professionals, each of whom offered precise instructions for finding a way around the stymie, going in-off or – in hopelessly 'snookered' positions – going bravely over the top. Bobby Jones illustrated this trick-of-the-trade shot in his classic book *Down the Fairway*. He advised the completely stymied player to use his mashie (5-iron) and let the natural loft elevate the ball just enough to clear the one in front. Employing an open stance, he came into the ball crisply, with a low-to-the-turf stroke without any lift or scoop. And I have always found it bewitching to study his illustrations and observe the ball's obedient little jump into the hole!

Abe Mitchell, reputedly the greatest golfer who never won the Open, recommended a mashie-niblick (7-iron) for the shorter-lofted shots, and a mashie or iron (3-iron) for longer distances. His diagrams illustrated stymies at varying distances from the hole and, if the offending ball was quite near, lofting directly into it!

However, one well-known professional and golf writer issued a warning about this shot. He said: 'If you live long enough, and play enough, you will one day pitch into the hole and see the ball bounce out again! That will be the time to summon your philosophy and assure yourself that it will all be the same a hundred years hence.' Do you wonder – going back to the questionnaire – at the ex-amateur and American Open champion saying: 'I like the stymie. Match-play is dull without it'? Seeing a little pitch pop into the hole, only to bounce perversely out again, was far from *dull*, I think. It would drive a few into hysterics!

The stymie was important enough to figure as a major shot of the game. It even appeared on the cigarette-cards of the day. I recall Pat Ward-Thomas writing of a curly-headed youth at Hindhead pictured on a card lofting over a stymie. This was none other than Dai Rees in his very early days.

Walter Hagen's choice of the greatest shot he ever played was a stymie. He was in a tight match-play situation against Abe Mitchell and said: 'On the twelfth green I played one of the finest stymies of my entire career. On his second shot Abe's ball was on the extreme back edge of the green. My shot was short and to the left. I played the third shot up and left myself eight feet from the hole. Abe had a thirty-foot putt and he all but holed it, just missing the cup and stopping on the very edge to the right, leaving me a dead stymie, blocking the hole.

'Things looked extremely black for me right then – having a dead stymie at eight feet and knowing if I didn't make it I'd be three down with only six more holes to play. I could putt around his ball, but I could see no possible chance to hole my ball. I decided to use a 7-iron. I looked the green over ... back and forth, back and forth. Then I hit my ball just short of Abe's, which lay delicately poised on the very rim of the cup. My ball hit a breath of an inch behind his, jumped it and stayed in the hole! We halved the hole and I was still in business. And that stymie shot of mine disturbed Abe so much he hooked his next tee shot badly, and lost the hole, leaving me only one down. I finished the match by winning 2 and 1. That stymie, the greatest shot I ever played, paid off.'

With Mitchell's ball on the lip of the hole, the dead stymie left Hagen's chances, to all intents and purposes, quite hopeless. But, as he had only the one stroke left for the half, he had nothing to lose and everything to gain. The miracle was that the ball went in. Harry Vardon, describing a similar situation, said: 'If the ball that stymies you is on the lip and your own is three yards away, it is obvious that you cannot pitch over it. From such a distance your own ball could not be made to clear the other one and drop again in time to fall into the tin.' Yet Hagen's *did*. A truly great shot, and Mitchell was only human in hooking wildly off the next tee. The surprising thing is that he hit the ball at all!

Reading of Hagen's shot may cause many old golfers to sigh at the stymie's death. It was an exciting part of match-play golf, and by its abolition a lot of spine-chilling drama has gone from the game. I recall Ronnie White, former English Amateur champion, playing in the Walker Cup match at Royal Birkdale, in 1951, being laid a dead stymie by Charlie Coe on the seventh green, yet dramatically lofting his ball into the hole. There have been equally successful spectacular shots, of course, but just think for a moment of Seve Ballesteros faced with a dead stymie in the Match-play Championship at Wentworth, or in the Ryder Cup matches. We can well imagine him following Hagen's wonderful shot, for here's a player after Hagen's own heart, a player with a flair for the impossible shot and the exquisite touch to achieve it.

Bobby Jones was a supporter of the stymie. He said it was a traditional part of match-play and should always remain so.

Even in 1961, he wrote an article 'The Stymie – Let's Have It Back', saying he was hopeful of its being restored to the game. 'It has been appalling to me to find that there are golfers of today who do not even know the meaning of "stymie",' he said. Bobby had every reason to remember the stymie and the part it played in his British Amateur win of 1930, the year he achieved the 'Grand Slam' of British and American Opens and Amateur Championships. Had it not been for a stymie at the 19th against Cyril Tolley, the unique record of four major titles might never have occurred. This is how Bobby described the play leading up to the dead stymie.

'Cyril Tolley and I are playing the first extra hole of an exciting match in which the strain on both players and a large gallery has been terrific. After two good drives I play the odd, a better-than-fair shot ten feet from the hole; Cyril plays a definitely slack second, off the green on the left. The chip is tricky, but again Cyril's shot is not good, seven feet short. I putt carefully, leaving my ball two inches from the hole, directly in Cyril's line, completely blocking the hole.'

Under today's rules, the ball nearer the hole would have been lifted and marked or conceded, and Tolley would have putted freely from seven feet for the half. Not a great distance for holing out. The match might then have gone on to the 20th, still open to the final outcome.

Jones argued that the stymie did not give him a lucky win. He considered he had played the hole better all the way, after the tee shot, and therefore was entitled to win it.

He concluded his article by recommending the return of the stymie as follows: 'With the stymie in the game, match-play golf becomes an exciting duel in which the player must always be on guard against a sudden, often demoralizing thrust. More than anything else, it points to the value of always being the closer to the hole on the shot to the green and after the first putt. The player who can maintain the upper hand in the play up to the hole rarely suffers from a stymie. In my observation, the stymie has more often been the means of enforcing a decision in favour of the deserving player, rather than the contrary. I think it merits a respected place in the game. I know a return to it would greatly enhance the interest and excitement of match-play golf for player and spectator alike.'

The word 'stymie' was not always understood. Thought to be

from 'styme', an old Scottish word meaning a minimum of vision or other things, it was sometimes humorously misinterpreted. We have all heard of the lady who went into Lillywhite's at Piccadilly Circus and tried to buy her husband a couple of dozen stymies for Christmas. I make no apology for mentioning her, nor for the story of the lady attending her first golf tournament. At a blind hole, her companion – well versed in the ways of the game – ran on ahead to find out where one of the shots had finished. Observing the player's ball sitting close to the flagstick, she shouted: 'My gosh, it's a dead stymie!' 'Ah!' exclaimed the first-timer, 'I thought I smelt something nasty as I came up the hill!'

44   *Looking at Logos*

Unpleasantness in the clubhouse bar again the other evening. The Old Codger was rabbiting on about logos in golf, which apparently are anathema to him, not only in the professional game but on the amateur scene as well. Never an easy chap to converse with, he was being particularly snotty with club members who – like a golfer who's just cut his tee-shot out of bounds – were doing their utmost to pretend they weren't there.

'Do any of you cloth-eared hackers know what a logo is?' he asked in the menacing manner of a prosecuting QC.

Dead silence ensued. Silence broken only by shuffling feet and creaking joints as the fellows round the bar practised their stances and elbow-bending, making out they hadn't heard him. None admitted to knowing what a logo was, of course, or to knowing anything at all about anything, if you know what I mean – wink, wink.

But then, from the corner of the room where it was darkest and impossible to identify the speaker, an anonymous voice said: 'A logo? Of course we know what it is. We also know what a no-go is. It's a place where we're told not to go-go.'

'I didn't ask about your damned no-go places,' exclaimed the Old Codger impatiently. 'I asked about logos.'

Well, you won't want me to go on too long about the Old Codger. We've heard him before, and the best thing would be to chloroform him and bundle him out of the way as quickly as possible, which will probably happen in the bar one day, as the speediest of quiet rebukes.

But – returning to his question – what is a logo? And what is its place in golf today?

A golfer unaware of the logo's distinguishing characteristics might be excused for believing it to be one of his shots that went terribly wrong by travelling in a low trajectory after being thinned and rocketing through the back of the green. In other

words, what might be called a 'low go'. Similarly, perhaps a boxer might look upon a logo as a wicked punch struck well below the belt. But – as most of us know already – a logo is simply a company emblem or message, and many well-known marketing concerns are aware that putting their logo on golf equipment is an effective way of promoting anything from banks to beers, petrols to pizzas, motor-cars to monkey-nuts.

On the professional tournament grind round the world's courses, it's commonplace for the golfer to distinguish himself from others by sporting his own distinctive logo or message. In America, especially, the golf pros wear their whiter-than-white head-visors with colourful slogans sponsoring commercial interests. Each tournament has its walking billboards of headgear, and as golf fans sit in front of TV screens and observe players playing their shots, it's often as intriguing for them to read the messages and advertisements as it is for the golfers to read the complexities of the putting surfaces.

As an example of this, many spectators have been completely foxed by messages on head-visors, and two spectators at a recent Open were overheard discussing David Graham's visor.

Curious as to what its message actually read, it was difficult, as he moved from shot to shot, for them to get the logo into proper focus.

'It says something about a *hangover*,' declared one, peering at the visor for all he was worth. 'It reads "MANUFACTURERS HANGOVER". I think it must be a joke. What he's saying is "Look at me, manufacturing great golf shots, with a terrible hangover." '

'Or does it mean the visor itself, actually hanging over his eyes?' asked the other.

But, of course, both explanations were hopelessly wrong. What Graham's visor read was 'MANUFACTURERS HANOVER', or 'Manny Hanny', as it's called, publicizing the New York City megabank that sponsors the annual Westchester Classic Golf tournament on the American PGA Tour.

'Manny Hanny' is but one of countless sponsors advertising on the American tour. Moreover, according to reports, professional golfers are paid thousands of dollars to wear visors and company logos, while keeping the sun out of their eyes and helping to build up the game's ever-growing reputation for commercialism. Leading players like Ray Floyd, Tom Kite, Peter Jacobsen – all Ryder Cup stars – are among those who have lucrative contracts for visors, bags and wearing apparel. Jim Thorpe, the coloured golfer, was the first player to wear the white, red-trimmed visor of 'Manny Hanny', and was reported to have been paid $10,000 for the service, though a figure of $2,000 is said to be more like the going rate.

British golf has similar logos on sweaters, balls and other familiar equipment. Logos on golf umbrellas are perhaps the best illustration, for many companies unconnected with golf are using this method of advertising. Quite apart from seeing them on every golf course, the umbrellas promote companies' logos and messages at almost every kind of sporting activity. When rain comes tumbling out of darkening skies, the ubiquitous golf umbrella opens up a colourful dome of advertising, often in the ordinary concourse of city and town.

The logo is into all sports. Lawn tennis is another sport punctuated by the logo. Leading players wear emblems on shirts and other equipment, and rules are in force governing the size of advertising on players' clothes, just as they are now in the Open. For example, in the Australian Open, Ivan Lendl,

Czechoslovakian world star, was fined $1,000 for wearing an oversized logo during the championships.

Amateur golfers are tempted to personalize their golf by having their names printed along tee-pegs and round the circumference of golf balls. Advertisements offer a wide range of personalized equipment – umbrellas, golf bags, club-covers, ball-markers, bag-tags, pitch-repairers, address labels for each shaft of the clubs and, on the American market, the speciality of a 24-carat gold-plated putter, jeweller-engraved with one's own name, golf club or corporate logo. Good value for the egotistical golfer at $79, postage paid and, for the guy who doesn't pay insurance on his clubs, much less cumbersome than fitting the putter with ball and chain.

Having one's name printed on tees and balls raises a number of delicate questions. For instance, what is one supposed to do after finding pegs or balls belonging to known club members? What's the etiquette? Section I of the Rules of Golf is no help, even though it goes to some length on etiquette. Should one play with the equipment regardless? Or simply hand it back? Perhaps the character of the chap standing with you is the criterion. If you don't particularly see eye-to-eye with him, well, you might be tempted to hang on. On the other hand, if you really like the guy, well, you, you, you – what I mean is – would this guy hand back any of your lost balls? Bernard Shaw's Eliza Doolittle has a neat answer to that.

But other pertinent considerations arise too, and the name on the ball might be the final arbiter. For example, a 'Beachcomber' name, like 'Charlie Suet' or 'Aubyn Spicecraft' would compel you to return the ball to its rightful owner – or throw it into the nearest pond. For who could feel inspired to compile a decent round, or score eagles or birdies, with 'Charlie Suet' printed on the ball? Other names that come to mind, from the golf writings of George Nash, are those of 'Lionel Nutmeg' and 'Ignatius Thudd.' If their personalized golf balls were found, they would have to be handed back, or perhaps slipped under a hen in the absence of china nest-eggs. R.G. Robertson-Glasgow once did that, and the next day found that the hen had laid an egg which was an exact fascimile of a golf ball in size and shape. Only the mesh markings were absent. He thought it would be pleasant to tee it up for a myopic and peppery golfer who was anxious to win for both personal and financial reasons.

Funny or perverse? Perhaps both. Rather like being drawn against Charlie Suet in, say, the Captain's Prize, and beating the living daylights out of him with his own lost ball.

Laying claim to a ball is no easy matter to prove. I recall many years ago a cartoon in *The New Yorker* which portrayed a golfer who had just driven out of bounds, together with a farmer who had picked up the ball in his field. They were standing either side of the field's fence disputing ownership. Over the top of his glasses, the farmer was studying the ball's identification, and saying: 'Mebbe 'tis. Mebbe 'tisn't. Your name Spalding?'

45   Something like a Duck

The 1982 Open Championship at Troon was remarkable not only for Bobby Clampett's lowest scoring over the first two rounds for almost half a century but also for the fact that, having completed the rounds, he compared himself to a duck.

Much as we were informed some years ago by Wodehouse that statisticians estimated that crime among good golfers was lower than in any class of the community except possibly bishops, so I'm prepared to state that there's no known instance of a golfer leading the Open field by five clear strokes comparing himself to a duck. Golf statisticians please note.

Commonplace enough in first-class and Test cricket, ducks hitherto have been complete strangers to championship golf. Yet Clampett's duck waddled in confidently as Clive Clark was interviewing the young phenomenon for BBC television following his record-breaking round of 66.

'You seemed very composed out there on the course today, Bobby. There was no sign of tension. Do you always find yourself able to play without too much tension creeping in?'

'Well, I think the best way to answer that,' said Bobby, 'is to tell you what someone once said about emotion and tension on the golf course. You see, it's something like a duck on a pond. It goes sailing along serenely over the surface without anyone being aware of all the paddling and steering going on under the water. I guess I'm something like that duck. Calm enough from outward appearances, but with an awful lot going on under the surface.'

As a charming example of an unexpected turn in the conversation, Clampett's remarks reminded me of Saki's short story in which someone walks into a tennis club saying: 'I know a man who has grown a potato weighing 2¼ pounds.' Now, pound-potato chats in changing-rooms seem about as momentous as those about ducks in Open Championship interviews.

However, the young American's analogy serves us well, for I doubt whether we could find a single golfer – amateur or professional – who doesn't do his very best to give onlookers the impression of being perfectly calm and collected, especially on the first tee. Yet however successfully he acts the part of a phlegmatic duck on an unruffled pond, there's always a fine collection of butterflies lurking under his belt!

'Make no mistake, Peter,' said Henry Cotton, as he and Alliss commented on TV as the Open competitors drove from the first tee, 'all these boys will be suffering from butterflies.'

Of all championship golfers, I should think Bobby Locke had the greatest reputation for unflappability. No matter what went wrong, his expression never changed. Hit or miss, on the green or off, in the hole or out, he never seemed to flap or lose his archbishop, cool-as-the-crypt demeanour. Relaxed as a pair of Victorian suspenders, he even appeared to be *enjoying* himself. Other players marvelled at him as a case-hardened, nerveless performer, impervious to bad lies and breaks.

That he was impervious to bad lies, I can personally verify. Playing in the Open at Royal St George's in 1949, one of his perfect drives finished in a deep, narrow divot mark, bang in the middle of the fairway. As we, his gallery, stood round the spot in commiserating silence, like mourners at the graveside, Bobby strolled up and saw his misfortune. Completely unperturbed, however, he gave a careful look at the place and then delighted us all by saying nonchalantly: 'Why didn't somebody kick it out?' Of course, those were in themselves easy-going days when spectators were allowed to walk the fairways and perhaps chat with the players or, if you were a lady watcher, identify their respective after-shave lotions.

Even so, I'm afraid Locke was by no means as phlegmatic as he would have had us believe. Listen to his *true* feelings and what he thought of his own temperament.

'I often laugh when people tell me, "You look so calm no matter how tense the game." I may look calm but frankly there are times when my stomach seems to be full of butterflies, but I try to camouflage my feelings so that my opponents do not know whether I am disturbed or not.'

Locke's outward calm was maintained by concentrating and

putting poor shots behind him immediately. 'What matters most is not the bad shot you have just made, but the good shot you are going to make next.'

This advice is similar to Harry Vardon's realization of the cold fact that, no matter what happened during a round, there was only one thing for him to do – keep on hitting the ball.

Another Bobby – Bobby Jones – had an altogether different analogy from Clampett's duck-on-a-pond. He viewed championships golf as something like being in a *cage*.

He said: 'Tournament golf! It's different from just golf in other ways, especially when it leads at last into the cage of championship. I read a line somewhere, or a title, "The Cage of Championship". It *is* something like that. Something like a cage. First you're expected to get into it, and then you're expected to stay there. But of course nobody can stay there. Out you go – and then you're trying your hardest to get back in again. Rather silly, isn't it, when golf – just golf – is so much fun?'

46 The Rise and Fall of Knickerbockers

Knicker-clad golfers the world over were braced up by the news that Bob Hope had donned a pair of natty knickers for the Hope classic, and thus given a much-needed lift to a nether garment that's been rather on the downward trend since South Africa's Bobby Locke raised knickerbockers to new heights in the forties and fifties.

The report from America said: 'This year Bob was outfitted in 1929 fashion, including knickers and Ben Hogan white cap. He tested a quip that he was Gene Sarazen's illegitimate son, found it elicited chuckles and stayed with it.'

If we take a long look backwards, we find that 1929 was a year of knickerbocker fever on the fairways. The immaculately clad Walter Hagen won the Open at Muirfield by no fewer than six shots, and not only did he do it in his knickers, but almost all the other leading players (Johnny Farrell, Leo Diegel, Abe Mitchell, Percy Alliss, Bobby Cruickshank) did it in their knickers as well. What's more, from 1926 on, all the Open winners were knickerbocker fanciers, right up to our own Henry Cotton, who sported them in his first Open triumph in 1934, even though in Britain they may have been known technically as plus-fours. All the more fitting then for Hagen, who was always a study in elegance, to wear his knickerbockers as he received the 1929 trophy from the Prince of Wales, also clad in knickerbockers. But that was not all. Hagen had won the previous year at Sandwich, and he and the Prince of Wales – and everyone else on the presentation platform – had sported the ubiquitous golfing knickers!

Gene Sarazen was rarely out of the reckoning in those years and, Open champion in 1932, rarely out of his favourite knickers, in which he was instantly recognizable. They became his trademark, and Bob Hope couldn't have chosen a more famous knickerbocker-Daddy than the popular Gene, known to golfers the world over as 'The Squire'.

Despite their popularity, knickerbockers were not without their enemies. No less a personage than H.G. Wells, famous novelist, reformer and controversialist, said that, 'The uglier a man's legs are the better he plays golf', and – as if that wasn't enough – he added that, 'A golfer's legs look especially beastly from behind.'

Perhaps Wells was just trying to be argumentative, as was his wont, for if we take the trouble to look at photographs of the older champions in their knickerbockers, their legs seem dashing and shapely enough and far from 'beastly'. Anyway, there were incontestable reasons for wearing knickerbockers and showing a leg, which Wells overlooked.

The greatest of all knickerbocker-wearing champions, Harry Vardon, refused to say very much on the criticial question of trousers versus knickerbockers, but he did tell us that he always wore knickers because they gave the utmost freedom to the ankle and leg, which he considered desirable. Harry made a lot of use of his ankles in his swing and so liked to have them as free as possible. He believed in screwing the left ankle into the proper position, and no pair of trousers was going to prevent his doing so. Vardon had strong views on keeping up his knickerbockers with the right kind of braces, too. Belts were out of the question. They gave the shoulders too much freedom.

However, whichever batch of old photographs we study – Abe Mitchell, Tommy Armour, Percy Alliss, Bobby Jones and Walter Hagen, the knickerbockers, diamond-patterned stockings, two-tone shoes and matching jackets are continuously there, with an air of seemliness and being suited to the occasion.

For example, I have an agreeable photograph of Bobby Jones and Walter Hagen shaking hands after their amateur-versus-professional match of 1926 (which Hagen won by 12 and 11 – 'We're still friends,' commented Bobby) that's full of knicker-bocker interest. Both are beautifully turned out in the style of the day, but with a very noticeable difference. Bobby's knickers are immaculately pressed down the *front* and Walter's down the *sides*. Which to choose? Which – if any – is taboo?

I make no pretence to an exhaustive knowledge of the proprieties of knickerbocker-pressing, but James Bond's $10,000 golf match against Goldfinger at Sandwich comes readily to mind. Readers of Ian Fleming's thriller will remember that 007 didn't like Goldfinger's plus-fours because they were too well cut and pressed down the sides! Yet here's the great Hagen, paragon and peacock of golfing plumage, also pressed down the sides! Of course, it's true that Walter had a fine disregard for the conventional, but I can't help thinking that Fleming wouldn't have put that bit in his novel if he'd seen this Hagen photograph. It's easily said that Goldfinger was incorrectly dressed, but quite outrageous to say the same of Hagen. Henry Cotton's a help here, for he's declared: 'I often wore striped plus-fours of the narrow kind, but unlike Abe Mitchell I did not favour a crease in mine, but in America it was considered well dressed to have a nice crease in one's plus-fours.' Perhaps, as the learned Doctor Johnson said: it's of no more matter where the crease is than what leg you put into your breeches first.

With the halcyon days of knickerbockers seemingly over, South Africa's Bobby Locke strolled majestically up the middle of the post-war fairways. 'Most people will have noticed that I always play in plus-fours,' he said. 'I find them the most comfortable form of golfing attire. To me golf and plus-fours are synonymous.' Like Sarazen, Bobby was instantly recognized in his knickers, white cap and white shoes, and his dress was so stylish that he destroyed at a single stroke of his hickory-shafted putter all those elderly, purple-nosed, pipe-smoking, plus-four golfers in the pages of *Punch*, who inanely asked one another how they were getting on and then replied: 'First-rate, old man. Just made three perfect putts on the last green.' Locke rarely, almost never, three-putted, and his knickers and old hickory putter were a sign of scientific economy on the green.

A major championship has not been captured by a knicker-clad golfer since 1957, when Locke won at St Andrews. A quarter of a century without a win is more than enough to get knickerbockers down. But they look back fondly to the great days of knickerbocker-champions and also take fresh heart from the modern young ladies who are doing such a great job in the back-to-knickerbockers movement by rushing into Harrods and Liberty's and suchlike places to buy them in black and gray and pin-striped wool – or whatever colour you care to think of – to wear jauntily around town. On the links, young ladies are bagging birdies in knickers, and each year sees them get more popular as a feminine golf wear, stylish and ideally suited to the game.

Yes. Knickerbockers are confident they'll rise again. As they say on the river, another Locke will be coming along soon. Meantime, Hope (with a capital H) is on their side. And where there's golf, there's Hope. And where there's Hope, there's knickerbockers.

A golfing character in Wodehouse nipped into a second-hand clothier's in the City to buy a putter which he spotted in the window, and came out with a suit of pink plus-fours that magically transformed his game. The proprietors of the establishment – name of Cohen Bros – also sold him the putter, a dog-collar, a set of dress-studs and a fireman's helmet, but when he wore the plus-fours he realized that for the first time in his golfing life he actually *looked like a golfer*. He'd discovered the secret at last – all you had to do was wear plus-fours!

Sadly, the pink plus-fours (made specially for Sandy McHoots, a former Open champion in Wodehouse's short story 'The Magic Plus-Fours') were set on fire as the hero was inside them. A box of matches ignited in his pocket and the poor devil had to jump into a pond to extinguish the flames. Perhaps the only recorded instance of golfing knickers being abandoned, charred and smouldering, under a bush at the 11th. A knickerbocker-wearer himself, Wodehouse obviously knew there was more magic in them than a pair of commonplace, uninteresting trousers.

47 Popping the Question

You won't believe this, I know, but the other day I had a letter from a young man who asked me if I thought the golf links a good place to ask a girl to marry him. 'She's a keen golfer, capable of playing a good game, and seems to have a womanly intuition and judgement for reading the line of a putt that is far superior to my own. She knows just how much to borrow without overdoing things so that putts are drawn magically into the hole.'

Naturally, I told him to propose to her at once. For any girl who knows just how much to borrow without overdoing it should make an ideal wife; added to which her ability to find the correct line on the greens would be invaluable to him as she pulled his trolley in important matches. Moreover, there's plenty of evidence that proposals of marriage have taken place on the links, often without a chap being expected to go down on his knees in the wet grass. But, just in case he doubted my word, I mentioned one or two distinguished authors of stories in which proposals of marriage took place.

'By the way, I'm going to propose to her tomorrow.'

'Already?'

'Can't put it off a minute longer. It's been as much as I could manage bottling it up till now. Where do you think would be the best place? I mean it's not the sort of thing you can do while you're walking down the street or having a cup of tea. I thought of asking her to have a round with me and taking a stab at it on the links.'

'You couldn't do better. The links – Nature's cathedral.'

Those who have read Wodehouse on golf will recognize the dialogue. It's a chap called Chester Meredith chatting with the Oldest Member about his intention to propose marriage to Felicia Blakeney (23, has a dog named Joseph, dances well and dislikes parsnips). Chester then loses no time in popping the

question and, though he fails at the first attempt, he succeeds at his second 'stab at it', mainly because of Felicia's admiration for his record-breaking golf. While the birds above them trill Mendelssohn's Wedding March, the newly engaged couple discuss the secret of golf as they stroll together over the scented Wodehouse meadows.

But Chester is worried. He tells Felicia that he's discovered the secret of golf. 'You can't play a really hot game unless you're so miserable that you don't worry over your shots. If you're really wretched, you don't care where the ball is going and so don't raise your head to see. Look at the top-notchers. Have you ever seen a happy pro?' Of course, Felicia (like us) has to admit she hasn't. And Chester's worry is that he's going to be so infernally happy from now on that he suspects his handicap will go up to 30 or something.

'Don't worry, precious,' says Felicia. 'Once we are married, I shall be able to think of at least a hundred ways of snootering you to such an extent that you'll be fit to win the Amateur Championship.'

'My angel,' cries Chester, as he folds her in his arms, using the interlocking grip.

One of Eric Linklater's novels has the golf links as the scene for a marriage proposal. The young man and his girl-friend slice their tee-shots into a belt of woodland and then conveniently plunge into the trees together. As they come upon their drives lying close beside an uprooted tree, the young man carefully hangs his clubs on a projecting branch and says slowly: 'I wonder if you would care to marry me?'

What I've always admired most in Linklater's young man is the careful way in which he hangs up his clubs. He doesn't just toss them down in an untidy heap in his eagerness to win the girl – as most scratch men might have done – but carefully suspends them on the branch of a tree. A methodical fellow, obviously, with a care for his equipment, even when, so to speak, he's as excited as a cat at a mouse show. One imagines him cleaning and buffing up his clubs later in the day, despite all the emotional strain he's been through. And I take pleasure in telling you that his proposal was accepted, for how could any decent girl with an eye to a tidy matrimonial home snatch a rug from under the feet of such a regular fellow?

Saki is yet another writer who gives us a proposal on the links. The young lady in the short story returns from a round of golf with her boy-friend in an elated state of mind to tell her mother of the marriage offer.

'It's all right about the proposal, he came out with it at the sixth hole. I said I must have time to think it over. I accepted him at the 7th.'

'My dear,' says her mother, 'I think a little more maidenly reserve and hesitation would have been advisable, as you've known him so short a time. You might have waited till the ninth hole.'

'The 7th is a very long hole. Besides, the tension was putting us both off our game. By the time we'd got to the ninth hole we'd settled lots of things. The honeymoon is to be spent in Corsica, with perhaps a flying visit to Naples, if we feel like it, and a week in London to wind up with.'

Bearing in mind that Saki wrote his short story more than seventy years ago, I think we must say that the young lady was a pretty fast worker in accepting her boy-friend's proposal at the seventh hole. A mere one hole spent thinking it over was pretty speedy stuff for those unenlightened times. But it makes one wonder how much faster a golfing girl of today would work. For example, if her boy-friend popped the question at the 6th (as in the Saki story), would she – assuming he had the honour and was on the point of driving off – (a) wait until he had driven, (b) accept before he reached the top of his backswing or (c) say 'Yes' in the middle of his waggle?

48   Lending a Hindering Hand

One of the latest teaching ideas from America touches upon a golfer's powers of concentration and temperament. In short, keeping one's mind on the job in hand and at the same time keeping one's cool. This is what's recommended.

'Get a friend – or friends – to play a practice round with you and give them permission to do anything they want to upset you. Tell them to move behind you as you tee off, sneeze while you're putting, make fun of your swing.'

Golfers are advised to treat this experiment as an inoculation to make them immune against outside influences that disturb concentration and thereby ruin their game. The idea is supposed to make them impervious to sudden movements and noise, and it is suggested that, when a friend has done his worst to cause whatever upset he can, the golfer himself should reciprocate with his own brand of heavy breathing and sneezing from behind the friend's swing.

So far so good. But, just in case we should be pounced upon to lend a hindering hand to fellow-golfers of disquieted nature, might it not be a wise precaution for us to give a little thought now to the sort of antics and noises that would be most off-putting (and therefore most helpful) during the golfer's swing? By so doing, we would gain a reputation as Mr Nasty himself, a guy, so to speak, well qualified in the art of turning sensitive golfers into gibbering idiots.

Perhaps you will agree that in an exercise of this kind, the element of *surprise* would be paramount. It would be useless to sneeze if the golfer we were trying to help was *expecting* a sneeze, and although the American idea advocates sneezing, such noise seems paltry and incapable of creating an immunity against being put off. Most of our opponents in the amateur game have been sneezing their heads off in conjunction with our swings for longer than we care to recall, and much more

dynamic interference will need to be thought up if we are to help our golfing friends achieve unbroken concentration and unflappable temperament.

To the element of surprise should be added that of secrecy. On no account should we let our friend know what's coming next. Also, it would help his cause if we could invent new and disturbing noises far removed from ordinary, run-of-the-mill sneezing, coughing, whistling, humming, knuckle-cracking, coin-jingling, club-dropping and sudden, top-of-the-swing cries like: 'Watch it, old chap! There's a bee on your ball!'

Commonplace plots of this sort would be no more likely to upset a golfer's swing than a sudden grunt would startle a golfing pig-farmer. What's needed is a large football-rattle hidden behind one's back, to be swung into action the moment the club starts down from the top. Or perhaps one of those duck-call things would fit the bill. Cleverly concealed in the palm of the hand, it could be blown suddenly to emit a paralysing 'Quark!' as the golfer attempted to knock in a crucial two-foot putt. These, together with other unsettling sounds, like frozen gooseberries dropped from shoulder-height onto a tin plate, should be used. Frozen gooseberries – though not yet part of golf gamesmanship – could cause an unsuspecting swinger to leap clean out of his spiked shoes. Loud snappings of spectacle-cases (the type that chop off a finger if one doesn't take care) could transform a phlegmatic golfer into a quivering jelly. Even a zip-fastener, adroitly used, could disrupt a swing. Indeed, the sound of a zip on a warm summer's day can cause more consternation than the bursting of a paper bag. What happens is that curiosity gets the better of the golfer. His concentration is broken by wondering who is undoing – and doing what – in close proximity to his swing. Yes. The quiet, insinuating sound of a zip can be as debilitating as the ominous crack of a wooden leg.

It's said that there's nothing new under the sun. Similarly, in the game of golf, there's little that's untrodden under the divot. Though this latest idea of friends co-operating to upset one another's swings by using ungentlemanly tactics may appear new, the deliberate upsetting of golfers has been experimented with before in tournament golf, rather than friendly practice sessions. I recall tournaments in the States that were held and strategically planned so that no competitor would be allowed to play good golf – if the organizers could possibly prevent it. Looked upon as a sort of duffer's revenge on the game, the tournaments brought into use numerous devices to wreck the competitors' golf by repeated interference. Tape recorders were hidden all over the course. When activated and loudly amplified, terrible noises came out of the woods. Sounds of cars crashing and sirens wailing. Elephants stampeding and screaming. Cannons booming at the first tee, timed precisely for the top of the backswing. Guitarists serenading golfers on the greens. Blaring bands, bagpipes, cymbals crashing and – as a humorous inconvenience – the amplified sounds of toilets flushing.

Trick golf balls that smoked and split in two when struck were palmed off surreptitiously to unsuspecting players. Faked old Scottish caddies, who declared they 'knew the course', were employed to give wrong lines for shots, so that even good drives disappeared into the woods.

'Why did you hit it in there? That's a forest,' complained the double-dealing caddie.

'But you *told* me to,' answered the golfer.

'You were supposed to *fade* the shot, not knock it into the goddamn woods.'

Almost every noise that could be thought of was tried out on the much-maligned golfers. Loudspeaker systems emitted animals' roars, machine-gun fire, steamboat hooting and miscellaneous music. A jazz band was set up on a cart and pulled round on a tractor. Soloists played and sang their way round the course. A hippie girl stood in the sand-traps and sang gentle ballads. A banjoist, old and topped off with a bowler hat many sizes too small for his head, strummed away far out on the course. Goats, cows, ducks, donkeys and chickens ate their fill on the fairways. A 300-pound turtle eyed the proceedings distastefully as he sampled the grass. The organizers called him a 'movable hazard', but the competitors thought he was merely a large boulder.

Even more way-out ideas included a Shetland pony painted with white stripes, masquerading as a zebra. A dress-shop dummy, clad in old clothes and a wide-brimmed hat, floating face-down at a waterhole. A llama running madly zigzag round the course. Stunt planes flying threateningly low over the fairways. Hot-air balloonists hovering above jeeps and amphibian vehicles. No known way of golfing sabotage was overlooked. Even so, despite all the flak and filibustering, someone managed to return a respectable 73 and another competitor achieved a hole-in-one.

In golf's early days, Horace Hutchinson wrote of the St Andrews golfer who made a match to play on level terms with a much stronger golfer, providing that he was permitted to say 'Booh!' three times during the round at the precise moment that his adversary was about to strike the ball. Pretending throughout that he was about to say 'Booh!', he stole up behind the golfer many times during the play, open-mouthed and menacing, yet never needed to use one of his 'Boohs!' Hanging like the sword of Damocles over his head, the mere threat of a 'Booh!' was enough to defeat the stronger player.

Perhaps, then, if we should be asked to lend a hindering hand to our golfing friends, it would be sufficient to stand behind them pretending we were on the point of bellowing a very loud 'Booh!'

If that blew their minds and barbecued their cool, we would know that we had lent a hindering hand with quiet and gentlemanly distinction.

49   The Longest Hole

In one of his golfing essays, Bernard Darwin wrote: 'One has often heard stories of cross-country feats and very seldom seen them. There is, for instance, a legend that an intrepid gentleman undertook to play from Maidstone to Littlestone, a distance of something over thirty miles. The feat involved the playing of shots through the public streets, a possible difference of opinion with the local authorities and, so history records, a loss of thirty-seven balls. How many thousand strokes he was allowed I do not know, but he won his bet. Let us hope it was a substantial one to compensate him for the loss of thirty-seven florins.'

So many years have passed since this golfing feat took place that a golf ball can no longer be purchased for a florin, a tenth of a pound or two-shilling piece. Today's golf ball costs the full pound, and often a good deal more, and had the intrepid gentleman used new ones he would have had to put his hand into his pocket to the extent of, say, £37. But Mr Darwin's facts about the playing of this hole were somewhat sketchy, as is indicated by a detailed account in *The Strand Magazine* of July 1913. The true story, under the heading of 'Marathon Golf – A Hole Thirty-five Miles Long', was written by T.H. Oyler, one of the golfers who actually took part in this unique event.

It was no lone golfer who undertook the task, but *two*, playing alternate shots. Morever, the bet was a far-from-substantial one of £5, arranged as a result of a party of golfers, living in the neighbourhood of Maidstone, returning from Littlestone where they had been golfing on the famous Kentish links. While waiting for their train, the question arose as to how many strokes would be needed to cover the distance from Maidstone to Littlestone. One of the party suggested that about 2,000 would be a fair number, whereupon a 'popular, sporting parson' wagered £5 that no one could do it in that number. The bet was

modest even in those days but would more than have covered the lost balls, as old re-painted ones were used.

The bet was promptly accepted by two of the party, and details were settled at once. The parson's only stipulations were: (a) that the match take place within three months; (b) that the ordinary rules of golf be observed; and that – as he was not prepared to journey on foot for so long a distance – (c) an umpire should be appointed to keep score. A 'well-known Cambridge undergraduate' promptly offered his services as the umpire but, the article added, 'Had he known the large amount of monotonous work attached to it, it is very doubtful if he would have accepted.' Darwin, a Cambridge golf Blue, would have had something to say about this, I think, had he had more details.

The match began in the early morning of a beautiful spring day at Linton Park, about three miles south of Maidstone, the squire of Linton, Mr F.S.W. Cornwallis, having given permission for the first shots to be played through his lovely park. But the standard of golf hardly matched the beauty of the morning, for the opening shot with a brassie landed in a rhododendron bush, out of which the players had to drop with a penalty stroke. The third shot also found the rhododendrons, and a quick switch was made from brassie to cleek in favour of more accuracy. Two or three brassies, cleeks and niblicks, together with driving-iron and mashie, and about 'half a gallon of old balls' newly painted for the occasion, were carried by the caddie. The cleek was in constant use until the cricket ground was reached, when it was thought safe to revert to the brassie once more. Trees in the lower part of the park marred the players' progress, until a niblick carried them over a high wooden fence into pastures beyond. Hedges frequently caused unplayable lies with consequent dropping and penalty stroke. On the sixty-fifth shot the ball disappeared into a river and was lost. Midday was reached with shot 158, which was driven on to the railway line at Hawkenbury Bridge, 'the spot where many years ago a disastrous accident happened to the boat-express in which Charles Dickens was a passenger'. In playing off the line, the ball hit a post and came back, and the niblick was resorted to again. Shot 213 brought the party to Headcorn at 2.30 p.m., and here a stump was stuck into the ground to mark the last stroke as the party retired to the village inn for lunch. On returning, they found that their caddie had mysteriously disappeared. Wheatfields and farms were crossed, as was the main Tenterden road on stroke 258, the ball having been recovered from a brickyard and a lie against a chicken-coop. On the Tenterden road the golfers attempted to run the ball along the road with cleek shots, but the scheme failed, as anything longer than a short putting stroke ran into ditches either side of the road.

Many hazards were met with along the way. Shots had to be played out of heaps of stones, thick willow-bushes and ditches, over stiles and through thickly-wooded countryside, where the ball rebounded from trees to a considerable distance. But the weather being dry and fields of wheat and oats well rolled, good brassie shots and distances were helpful. Across rough arable land the going was very difficult, and the niblick was the only club that could be played successfully. Just before six o'clock the players pitched into a farmyard, had some trouble in getting out and decided to insert their marking-stump and call it a day. Their position was close to Crampton House Farm, between Biddenden and High Halden, and they had covered about fourteen miles in 427 strokes.

The following morning was a repeat of the previous day's frustrations. Hedges and ditches, woods and meadows, roads and farms, all were tackled with a variety of shot-making, but an unexpected rebuff was met with in the middle of a small meadow, when the owner, rushing up, demanded to know what they were doing on his premises. They replied that they were playing golf (as though that explained everything!), and he requested them to go away as quickly as possible. 'Fortunately a capital brassie shot into a rough wheat-field took us on to another farm, and peace was restored.' However, at this point, their caddie was involved in a row with another lad, was dismissed, and another engaged.

Cross-winds made the going very tiring, and many awkward lies were experienced. A sliced ball pitched into a hop-garden in which the poles stood so close together that effective golf swings could not be made. But a niblick landed the ball into a wood and some good brassie shots were made in a large field of rolled oats. The 500th stroke was greeted with an interval for refreshments.

Further progress slowed considerably, owing to dykes of water which were too wide to jump. The golfers often had to retrace their steps several hundred yards to find gateways, resulting in a belated lunch at Appledore at 4.25, instead of an anticipated 2.30. Their score at this stage was 714.

After another change of caddie and the knocking of shot 718 into a canal, there was trouble with rushes and ditches, and then getting onto a road and hitting a house; but the Railway Hotel was reached, which they hit with their 785th stroke. Tea was taken at 5.50 and, refreshed, they putted over the railway-crossing, having first hit the gate and bounced onto the rails. The staff of the Appledore station stood in amazement as the ball was played from the middle of the track.

The players now realized that they were well within their allotted strokes and wisely kept to the road for a while, afterwards branching off through oats, beans and pasture. Shot 842 was lost in a wide dyke; 844 shared the same fate and, as the dyke was too wide to jump, a halt was called for the night. The peg driven, they walked to the station and caught a train for Lydd, where they spent the night.

The following morning brought them to Brenzett, on the 915th stroke, after crossing pasture, arable, oats, wheat, and many waterways too wide to jump. Here, a friend offered sloe gin, which greatly assisted progress, brassie shots flying far and sure for a time. Reaching Romney Marsh, they twice hit a sheep and were frequently and frustratingly in small ditches, rushes and reeds, requiring a succession of shots of little distance. On the 1,000th stroke the ball hit a tree, but soon afterwards the water-tower at Littlestone was sighted and a bee-line made for it through sandhills and rabbit-holes, in one of which they lost a ball.

Arrangements had previously been made with the Littlestone Golf Club for the marathon golfers to hole out on the first green of the links, which they did at 11.38 a.m. on the third day of their journey across countryside hazards, with their 1,087th stroke. A good mashie shot had put them on the green within four feet of the longest hole in golf and, having been in many diverse holes along the way, they had finally found the one they were aiming for to win their bet.

In summing up, for several days afterwards the players were very tired, particularly in the arms, hands and wrists, caused by striving for as much distance as possible on all shots. They used a compass and a good personal knowledge of the area for finding their way across thirty-five miles of countryside; but even so, many detours were found necessary to avoid woods, hop-gardens, marshes and arable land. The dry weather and the rolled cornfields saved hundreds of strokes, for a niblick and many more strokes would otherwise have been required. Only seventeen balls were lost (an exceedingly small number and one at variance with Darwin's thirty-seven), and 62 had to be dropped with consequent stroke penalties. Several papers reported the feat, and in one daily the reporter said he was reminded of 'those semi-legendary runs of the old Welsh hounds in the days when we are told they used to run a fox the whole of one day, then turn in for the night at the nearest farmhouse, and take up the running again with the dawn of the next day.'

Throughout the journey, caddies were a recurring difficulty and, in all, six or seven were employed, each one going only a few miles before wanting to return, for fear of getting lost.

Such a marathon attempt today would, one feels, be much more problematic. Crossing railways, playing shots from between the lines or along traffic-infested roads would be well-nigh impossible. Traffic wardens and protest groups, and owners of land one attempted to cross, would surely respond unfavourably, as would hotel-keepers called upon to provide lunch at 4.25 p.m. instead of the anticipated 2.30. Sloe gin, I fear, would be much slower in making its welcome intervention in play.

Statistically minded readers might be interested to know that the hole was 61,600 yards long, par 1,087, and the average distance of shot 56.669733 yards.

50 The People Behind

Like the porpoise and the whiting in *Alice in Wonderland*, the people behind us on the golf links are sometimes too close for comfort and, so to speak, are treading on our tail. A hot-foot lot, they're every bit as disconcerting and detestable as the people in front who, going along at only snail's pace, hold us up vexatiously.

Bernard Darwin wrote passionately of the people in front. 'They waggle for hours; they stroll rather than walk; they dive into their monstrous bags in search of the right club and then it is the wrong number. Their putting is a kind of funereal ping-pong.' His essay 'The People in Front' concludes with these golfers standing in the middle of the green having taken out 'a horrid little card and pencil' to 'write down their horrid little score' and, in his mind's eye, Darwin is moved to let out a blaring yell of 'Fore!' and so make them duck and cower for their lives. 'They may think us ill-mannered,' he says, 'but what does that matter? The worst they can do is to write an article about the people behind.'

Patrick Campbell once had the unusual experience of playing with a beginner who threw down his bag, turned to face the people behind and roared 'Fore!' 'It was the first time I'd ever heard the cry in, as it were, reverse,' he said.

But why – when we ourselves are the people in front being harassed by the players behind – is it not possible to let loose an appropriate yell in reverse? 'Fore!' is out of place, of course. 'Wait!' or 'Stay!' or, perhaps better still, a loud authoritative 'Sit!' in bossy Barbara Woodhouse doggy-style might have the desired effect. That we should be more than justified in making the shout, there's not the slightest doubt. After all, it's not *we* who are playing too *slowly*. It's *they* who are playing too *quickly*. And having said that, one can't help pausing to ask why it is that no one is ever accused of playing golf too quickly.

Like inconsiderate beetles that alight on our ball just as we are about to hit it, the people behind know as little of our world as we know of theirs. If they accuse us of playing too slowly, should we not counter-accuse them of playing too quickly? Are we to blame if they haven't the gumption to toss up a few bits of grass to assess the force or way of the wind? And are they not foolhardy to strike their putts without a glance at the line and the tricky undulations of the green? Are we to be expected to forgo these finer arts and subtleties of the game, merely to let the people behind go through?

No! 'Sit!' we should boom loudly in reverse. Before committing ourselves to putting, let's make sure the borrow is 9½ inches to the right. Anyone (except the peasants behind) can see this is a switchback green running in all directions at once.

Thoughtless golf is bad golf. Golf played too quickly invariably winds up as a card full of six and sevens repented at leisure.

The people behind are sometimes in so much of a lather they would deny us the time to climb into waterproofs in sudden showers of rain. Umbrellas they eschew. They have never heard of drying hands and grips on a towel. Golf gloves – like their wife's garden – they do not dig. All they want is to press on. Why, if the truth were known, they probably don't even notice it's raining!

There are people behind who are wise in the ways of *not* going through, even if you invite them to do so. They know that on unfamiliar courses the people in front act as a pilot and show others the way. This is especially so in early morning, misty conditions, for only local members can smell out the line to take. So the people behind follow on gratefully. It's a ploy that makes play possible when there would be no play at all.

The gentlemanly locals may ask: 'Would you care to go through? We're a four, and you're only two. We don't wish to hold you up.'

'No, thanks,' say the people behind. 'We'd be lost without someone in front. Please carry on.'

So the people behind are still the people behind and are thankful for it. Those in front melt away into the hazy distance to form four shadowy, invaluable marker-posts. The people behind aim their shots at these ghostly figures and pray their insurance cover is fully paid up. 'Did Kathy settle with The Man from The Pru?' As the tee shots fly forward, ears are pitched to catch any sudden whimpering cry or agonized shout, as of someone thumped by a 1.68 many-dimpled, high-velocity missile.

Not all of the people behind are evilly inclined. Some are both kind and considerate. They return our cherished Johnny Revolta sand-iron that we absent-mindedly left behind alongside the fifth green, or perhaps hand back a club cover, ball sponge or beer-stained deerstalker hat. And of course we are eternally grateful to them. Why, the people behind have even been known to ask if we lost a brand-new Titleist just off the thirteenth fairway.

Of course we did, and many thanks! What a sheer joy these charming and scrupulously honest golfers are. The people behind ...

A Golfer's Bibliography

The following works are among many which have been helpful in writing the articles collected in *This for the Half*. They are listed as acknowledgement to their authors and as a guide to readers who may wish to seek further reference.

A-Sitting on a Gate, Ben Travers (W.H. Allen, 1978)

Best of Henry Longhurst, The, edited by Mark Wilson and Ken Bowden (Collins, 1979)

Bogey Man, The, George Plimpton (André Deutsch, 1969)

Common Touch, The, James Agate (Chapman & Hall, 1926)

Complete Golfer, The, Harry Vardon (Methuen, 1928)

Down the Fairway, R.T. Jones and O.B. Keeler (Allen & Unwin, 1927)

Express and Admirable, James Agate (Hutchinson)

Fallodon Papers, Viscount Grey (Constable, 1928)

Gallery of Women Golfers, A, Enid Wilson (Country Life, 1961)

Game of Golf, A, Francis Ouimet (Hutchinson, 1933)

Game's Afoot, The, Bernard Darwin and others (Sidwick & Jackson, 1926)

Golfer's Companion, The, Peter Lawless (Dent, 1937)

Golf is my Game, Bobby Jones (Chatto & Windus, 1961)

Golf Omnibus, The, P.G. Wodehouse (Barrie & Jenkins, 1973)

Golf's No Mystery, R.A. Whitcombe (Dent, 1938)

Letters of a Modern Golfer to his Grandfather, Henry Leach (Mills & Boon, 1910)

Mad Ducks and Bears, George Plimpton (Random House, New York, 1973)

Miss Mapp, E.F. Benson (Hutchinson, 1933)

Modern Fundamentals of Golf, The, Ben Hogan with Herbert Warren Wind (Nicholas Kaye, 1957)

Mostly Golf, edited by Peter Ryde (Adam & Charles Black, 1976)

My Golfing Life, Alexander Herd (Chapman & Hall, 1923)

Old Friends, Andrew Lang (Longmans, Green, 1913)

Orange Tree, The, Robert Lynd (Methuen, 1926)

Perfect Golfer, The, H.N. Wethered (Methuen, 1931)

Playing the Like, Bernard Darwin (Chapman & Hall, 1934)

Round with Darwin, A, edited by Margaret Hughes (Souvenir Press, 1984)

Rubs of the Green, Bernard Darwin (Chapman & Hall, 1936)

Shorter Ego, A, James Agate (Harrap, 1945)

Sixty Years of Golf, Robert Harris (Batchworth Press, 1953)

Sport of Princes, The, Laddie Lucas (Stanley Paul, 1980)

Strand Magazine, The, George Newnes, 1913

Walter Hagen Story, The, Walter Hagen with Margaret Seaton Heck (Heinemann, 1957)

Way to Golf, Harry Weetman (Ward Lock, 1953)

With Prejudice, Gerard Fairlie (Hodder & Stoughton, 1952)

World That Fred Made, The, Bernard Darwin (Chatto & Windus, 1955)

Index

All Sphere Books are available at your bookshop or newsagent, or can be ordered from the following address: Sphere Books, Cash Sales Department, P.O. Box 11, Falmouth, Cornwall TR10 9EN.

Please send cheque or postal order (no currency), and allow 60p for postage and packing for the first book plus 25p for the second book and 15p for each additional book ordered up to a maximum charge of £1.90 in U.K.

B.F.P.O. customers please allow 60p for the first book, 25p for the second book plus 15p per copy for the next 7 books, thereafter 9p per book.

Overseas customers, including Eire, please allow £1.25 for postage and packing for the first book, 75p for the second book and 28p for each subsequent title ordered.